FIGHTING BACK

*To my parents, Frank and Helen, who succeeded
as parents and examples in ways they
may not even have suspected.*

—R. D.

*To my parents, Arthur, Sr. and Phyllis,
who taught me to approach life with my feet on the ground,
my face with a smile, my eyes straight ahead,
and my arms wide open. All my love.*

—A. L.

FIGHTING BACK

BACK

Neighborhood
Antidrug
Strategies

Robert C. Davis
Arthur J. Lurigio

SAGE Publications
International Educational and Professional Publisher
Thousand Oaks London New Delhi

For information address:

 SAGE Publications, Inc.
2455 Teller Road
Thousand Oaks, California 91320
E-mail: order@sagepub.com

SAGE Publications Ltd.
6 Bonhill Street
London EC2A 4PU
United Kingdom

SAGE Publications India Pvt. Ltd.
M-32 Market
Greater Kailash I
New Delhi 110 048 India

Printed in the United States of America

Library of Congress Cataloging-in-Publication Data

Davis, Robert C. (Robert Carl)
    Fighting back: Neighborhood antidrug strategies / authors, Robert
C. Davis, Arthur J. Lurigio.
        p. cm.
    Includes bibliographical references and index.
    ISBN 0-8039-7112-5 (acid-free paper).—ISBN 0-8039-7113-3 (pbk.:
acid-free paper).
    1. Narcotics, Control of—United States—Citizen participation.
2. Drug abuse and crime—United States. 3. Crime prevention—United
States—Citizen participation. I. Lurigio, Arthur J.
II. Title.
HV5825.D38 1996
363.4′5′0973—dc20   95-41798

This book is printed on acid-free paper.

96 97 98 99 10 9 8 7 6 5 4 3 2 1

Sage Production Editor: Tricia K. Bennett

Contents

1. Introduction

The use of illegal drugs, particularly cocaine, became the focus of domestic public policy during the latter half of the past decade. It became difficult to switch on television or pick up a newspaper without encountering a horrific story about violence connected to the drug trade or attempts by government or citizens to fight back. The public concern spawned a federal war on drugs and significant increases in criminal justice spending at the state and local levels.

The massive amounts of government dollars spent on interdiction, apprehension, prosecution, incarceration, treatment, and public education apparently had some effect. According to the National Institute on Drug Abuse National Household Survey on Drug Abuse, use of illicit drugs has been on the decline since the mid-1980s (see Figure 1.1).

Yet in spite of more than a decade of strenuous efforts by federal, state, and local governments, illicit drugs continue to pose a serious challenge to society. For example, in 1993,

- An estimated 1.1 million persons were arrested for sale, manufacture, or possession of drugs.

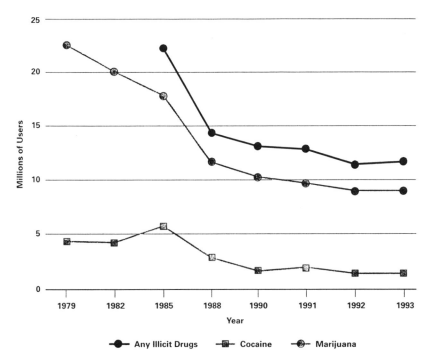

Figure 1.1. Past-Month Use of Any Illicit Drugs, Marijuana/Hashish, and Cocaine, 1979-1993
SOURCE: White House (1995).

- Nearly half a million drug-related medical emergencies occurred nationwide. More than one third of AIDS infections are associated with drug use.
- Federal, state, and local governments spent $25 billion on drug enforcement. (White House, 1995)

There are disturbing trends today that require us to maintain our efforts to control the sale of illegal drugs. Although the number of drug users has dropped since the mid-1980s peak, the decline has been in casual users. The number of hard-core users (persons who use illicit drugs at least weekly and who exhibit behavioral problems stemming from drug use) has shown no such decline (see Figure 1.2). As a result of these trends, drug use has increasingly become

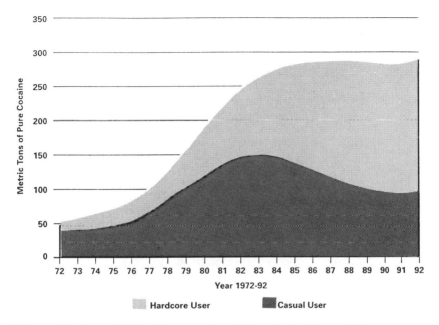

Figure 1.2. Annual U.S. Consumption of Cocaine by Type of User,
1972-1992
SOURCE: White House (1995).

associated with urban poverty, desperation, and crime. Moreover,
data show that one in five high school seniors has used drugs on a
regular basis, and the proportion of young people using drugs is
increasing (White House, 1995).

In this book, we focus on one aspect of the continuing battle
against illegal drugs. We do not discuss federal efforts at interdicting
the supply of drugs, state efforts to rehabilitate drug addicts, or even
local efforts to disrupt citywide supply networks. Rather, we look at
what is being done by partnerships of law enforcement and grassroots citizen groups at the most basic level—the neighborhood—to
prevent and discourage small-time drug retailers from practicing
their trade. We begin with a discussion of drugs and the urban
ghettos of the United States where they have developed such an
intractable hold on the life of communities.

Drug Use in Inner Cities

Forty years ago, severe racial prejudice kept African Americans and other minorities from fully participating in U.S. society. Despite the pernicious effects of racism, most minority residents in inner cities had homes, steady incomes, and a variety of other social supports. Furthermore, although the job opportunities available to African American men were in lesser-paying positions, such men were only somewhat less likely than their white counterparts to be employed (Johnson, Williams, Dei, & Sanabria, 1990).

With the advent of the civil rights movement, the force of law was brought to bear on the side of minorities seeking equal access to jobs, housing, education, and other opportunities. Yet years after the legal status of inner-city minorities had radically improved, their living conditions grew steadily worse. By the mid-1980s, the jobless rate among minorities had doubled, and half of all African American children lived in single-parent families with a poverty rate of more than 90% (Freeman & Holzer, 1986; Gibbs, 1988). The number of affordable homes dramatically decreased and many low-income families became homeless (Ropers, 1988).

The decline in quality of life among inner-city residents has many, varied causes. One contributing factor is widespread illegal drug use and sales. Heroin use gained a significant foothold in African American communities as early as the 1950s, following a flood of immigration from the rural South to the urban North (Courtwright, 1986). It became more pervasive in the 1960s and early 1970s, coinciding with the growth of the drug culture, the return of heroin-addicted Vietnam war veterans, and the increased incidence of urban riots (Hunt & Chambers, 1976).

Heroin use declined in the 1970s, but cocaine use spread among inner-city youth just as it had earlier among wealthier segments of U.S. society (Johnson, Williams, et al., 1990). A new technique for preparing cocaine, developed in Los Angeles in the early 1980s, made it even more popular and inexpensive by purifying it into smokable "rocks," or "crack" (Siegel, 1982). By the mid-1980s, cocaine use had exploded in major cities. Drug cases overwhelmed the courts, hospital admissions for drug overdoses soared, and the number of treatment slots could not accommodate the number of persons seeking drug rehabilitation (Smith, Davis, & Goretsky, 1991). According to Trebach and Inciardi (1993),

> For the inner cities across America, the introduction of crack couldn't have happened at a worse time. The economic base of the working poor had been shrinking for years, the result of a number of factors, including the loss of many skilled and unskilled jobs to cheaper labor markets, the movement of many businesses to the suburbs and the Sun Belt, and competition from foreign manufacturers. . . . Without question, by the early to mid-1980s, there was a growing and pervasive climate of hopelessness in ghetto America. (p. 175)

The Link Between Drugs and Crime

The rate of violent crime climbed dramatically in the inner cities in the 1980s as drug sales and use increased. Drugs and crime are associated in three basic ways. First, the intoxicating and disinhibiting effects of drugs can encourage criminal behavior. Second, the fact that drug use is illegal creates a black market, which leads to violence among dealers and corruption among law enforcement officials. Third, drug users may commit crimes to support their habits. The second and third connections do not stem from drug abuse per se but from drug policies that emphasize prohibition and enforcement, which drive up the price of drugs and force users to turn to crime and dealers to turn to violence to protect their business interests (Nadelman, 1988). Thus, both drugs and drug laws cause crime (Boyum & Kleiman, 1995).

Other factors may explain the association between drug use and crime. Both behaviors may be part of a deviant subculture that promotes indifference to risk and rule breaking. Income-generating crime may support drug use by giving drug-involved offenders the money to spend on their habits (Boyum & Kleiman, 1995). Nearly two thirds of the convicted jail inmates participating in a national survey, however, reported that they committed their current offenses for reasons other than needing drug money. Other studies suggest that drug use may intensify and perpetuate criminal activity but rarely causes a person to commit crimes. Most street criminals were involved in crime before they engaged in drug use (Ball, Rosen, Flueck, & Nurco, 1981; Inciardi, 1980; Nurco, Kinlock, & Balter, 1993).

Serious drug users tend to commit a disproportionate number of crimes (e.g., Chaiken & Chaiken, 1982; Nurco, Ball, Shaffer, & Hanlon, 1985). Although overall drug abuse in the United States declined in 1993, it remains at a high level among criminal offenders (Schmalleger, 1995). The Drug Use Forecasting (DUF) program of the National Institute of Justice, through which drug use of new arrestees has been monitored in 23 U.S. cities since 1987, showed in 1993 that 54% to 81% of male arrestees tested positive for at least one illicit substance. Across all DUF sites, drug use was most prevalent among men charged with drug sales or possession, assault, burglary, robbery, and theft (National Institute of Justice, 1994).

Similarly, high rates of drug use appear among prison inmates and parolees. Close to half of the nation's state prisoners reported using illicit drugs before their most recent arrests (Innes, 1988). The majority had never been in drug treatment programs and many began using drugs during adolescence. A subset of these prison inmates could be classified as high-rate, dangerous, drug-involved offenders who had committed crimes for several years before being arrested and sentenced to prison for the first time (Chaiken, 1986).

Anglin and his associates (e.g., Anglin & Hser, 1990; Anglin & Speckart, 1988) have found that criminal activity among heroin addicts coincides with periods of increased drug use. Conversely, when addicts participate in drug treatment programs their criminal activity diminishes, at least for the duration of the program. In addition, drugs are implicated in at least a third of the homicides in New York City (Goldstein, 1985), including those in which the perpetrator was under the influence of drugs (accounting for 25% of total homicides) and those in which people were murdered as a direct consequence of the illicit drug trade (accounting for 10% of total homicides).

Impact of Drugs on Communities

Drug sales and the crimes they may spawn have affected every major U.S. city. Drugs have had especially detrimental effects on poor neighborhoods and are both a symptom and a cause in the continued decline of those areas (Johnson, Williams, et al., 1990).

Drugs in inner-city communities have created a criminal underclass involved heavily in drug distribution, sales, and consumption. Members of this underclass often engage in violent and disruptive behaviors that have had a devastating impact on the poor (Johnson, Williams, et al., 1990). Scholars have compared the psychological consequences of living in underclass neighborhoods to the effects of living in a war zone (Garbarino, Kostelny, & Dubrow, 1991). In a 1988 national survey of poor households, 40% of the respondents identified illegal drugs and drug problems as the Number 1 issue facing the nation (Lavrakas, 1988). Similarly, a national survey of law enforcement executives indicated that citizens in their jurisdictions considered drug trafficking the country's principal crime problem (Lavrakas & Rosenbaum, 1989).

Drug sales provide poorly educated, unemployable, and impoverished youths with a steady "job" that is easy to learn, highly profitable, and relatively low risk in terms of arrest and incarceration (Johnson, Kaplan, & Schmeidler, 1990). Drug habits may force young men and women into prostitution or drug sales. An entire generation of inner-city inhabitants are being lured away from mainstream employment into the drug trade, which leads many to prison or premature death. In short, the drug trade has had destructive effects on people's lives: It introduces them to crime as a way of life, increases their risk for drug abuse, and attenuates their prospects for legitimate employment (a record of arrests and prison time precludes their obtaining jobs). All these factors make it more likely that they will commit crimes outside the drug business (Boyum & Kleiman, 1995).

There seems to be a relationship between drugs and neighborhood disintegration (Clayton, 1981; Gandossy, Williams, Cohen, & Harwood, 1980; Inciardi, 1986). Citizens typically perceive visible drug sales and use as signs of social disorder and degeneration

(Skogan, 1990). When residents become acutely aware of active drug dealers and prospering "drug houses," they conclude that citizens and the police have lost control over the streets. Residents soon begin to view their community as an inadequate environment in which to raise children and to establish businesses.

Neighborhoods with high levels of social disorder (e.g., public drinking and drug use, drug sales, corner gangs, street prostitution, panhandling, verbal harassment of women, open gambling) and physical decay (e.g., vandalism, trash in vacant lots, boarded-up buildings, stripped and abandoned cars) have significantly higher crime rates and fear of crime. These factors, collectively referred to as *incivilities* (Hunter, 1978), may be indirectly linked to crime through their effect on residents' fear (Skogan, 1988, 1989). For example, Taylor and Gottfredson (1987) propose a causal sequence in which incivilities lead to fear of crime, which leads to lower levels of informal social control, which lead to more crime and more fear. Similarly, Wilson and Kelling (1982) suggest that fear of crime causes community residents to be less vigilant, more suspicious of their neighbors, and less likely to become involved in collective anticrime activities. Consequently, the neighborhood becomes "vulnerable to criminal invasion." The appearance of incivilities in neighborhoods covaries with crime in a predictable pattern. Areas with the highest crime rates are characterized by more garbage, gangs, abandoned buildings, drug dealing, and empty lots than neighborhoods with the lowest crime rates.

Drugs are responsible for decreases in neighborhood viability and for the flight of families from inner-city communities. Based on research in Philadelphia, Rengert (1990) reports that property crimes cluster around locations where drugs are sold. Furthermore, drug sales, with their attendant crime and violence, make residents reluctant to use outdoor spaces, causing the neighborhood to become less safe and less conducive to family life. Residents who are financially able to leave the neighborhood do so, resulting in plummeting property values and abandoned houses. The social fabric of the community is ultimately destroyed.

Rengert's argument is consistent with general theories about the effects of disorder on community decline, which we noted earlier:

Drugs and other signs of social and physical disorder convey a message to residents and outsiders alike that a neighborhood is unsafe. Fear among residents is heightened and a downward spiral of crime, fear of crime, and neighborhood deterioration is triggered (Skogan, 1990; Wilson & Kelling, 1982).

Drugs have also reinforced the subculture of violence that exists in impoverished neighborhoods (cf. Wolfgang & Ferracuti, 1967). The rate of violent crimes climbed precipitously during the 1980s as drug sales and use increased. Much of the recent upsurge in inner-city drug violence is related to the particular circumstances surrounding the crack trade, which differentiate it from other illegal drug businesses, such as very young dealers and curbside sales (Hamid, 1990).

In some cities, violence among drug dealers is rampant. Possession and sale of drugs are illegal so business arrangements between dealers and between dealers and customers are not governed by law. Violence is the mechanism for resolving disputes over territory or disagreements about the quantity or quality of drugs. Violence is also the preferred means for punishing recalcitrant employees or customers who renege on their payments (Boyum & Kleiman, 1995). But as Boyum and Kleiman point out,

> It is not clear how much of the violence among drug dealers is attributable to the drug trade itself, as opposed to the propensities of the individuals employed in it or the economic, political, social, or cultural conditions of drug-impacted communities. Violent drug dealers tend to live and work in poor, inner city neighborhoods, where violence is common, independent of the drug business. (p. 299)

Fagan and Chin (1990) argue that violence among drug dealers may be expressive or may be used as a means of social control. These authors argue that both types of violence are more common among crack cocaine dealers than among sellers of other drugs: Cocaine sellers are "more likely than other sellers to use violence for economic regulation and control, but also more likely to use violence in other contexts" (p. 36).

Conceptualizations of Drug Markets

Economic Approaches. According to one view of drug markets, drug selling and buying can be described in the same terms that are applied to legal businesses. Transactions in drug markets are governed by the basic principles of prices and quantities (Kleiman & Smith, 1990): Prices go up as quantities available for sale decline, and consumers purchase greater quantities when prices are low.

Drug markets also exhibit unique features. Moore (1973, 1976) hypothesized that retail purchases of illegal drugs are influenced not only by the prices of the drugs but also by what he termed "search time." This includes the time to find a drug dealer and the risks of being arrested, robbed, or cheated while buying drugs or poisoned by taking drugs. These nonmonetary costs may be as important in influencing people's decisions to purchase drugs as the actual prices of the drugs themselves. Another unique feature of drug markets is that increases in the costs of illegal drugs do not usually result from the prices set by producers, importers, or high-level distributors. Rather, most of the added costs come from low-level retailers (Kleiman, 1992).

Drug-Selling Organizations. Some researchers have focused on the ways that persons engaged in drug sales are organized. Initial accounts of crack cocaine selling suggested that youth gangs involved in the business were becoming more entrepreneurial and more highly organized (Johnson, Williams, et al., 1990; Skolnick, 1990). Loosely organized youth gangs were seen as evolving into corporate drug-dealing gangs (Taylor, 1990).

Later researchers disputed the view that drug dealing is controlled by organized crime (Mieczkowski, 1990). They report that in the markets they examined, most drug-dealing gangs are loosely organized, and freelance drug sales predominate (e.g., Decker, 1993; Esbensen & Huizinga, 1993; Joe, 1992; Waldorf & Lauderback, 1993). These researchers characterize drug dealing as a "semi-organized response of young people to decreased opportunities in the postindustrial era" (Hagedorn, 1994, p. 291).

Most recently, researchers have suggested that drug selling takes on different forms depending on local conditions. Neighborhood context (factors such as ethnicity, homogeneity, local political organization, and physical ecology of drug markets) appears to play a significant role in determining the way in which drug selling is conducted and the extent to which strong, centralized organizational structures emerge (Fagan, 1992; Hagedorn, 1994).

Ecology of Drug Markets. Buerger (1992) argues that drug markets exhibit different forms intended to reduce risk of penetration. He describes four types of primary drug-selling organizations: *Clubs* exercise the most stringent screening, selling only to known customers. Because only members can purchase drugs at a club, they are difficult for police to penetrate. *Speakeasies* require potential buyers to provide code words or signals to gain admission. *Drive-ins* use intermediaries to carry money and drugs from buyer to seller. *Dealerships* use intermediaries to screen potential buyers and then bring the buyer to an indoor location to complete the sale with a higher-up.

Each of Buerger's four primary defensive strategies can be used in different kinds of markets, ranging from *drug bazaars* where large numbers of buyers and sellers exchange drugs in outdoor public spaces, to *cuckoo's nests* in vacant or borrowed indoor locations, to *rotation systems* with constantly changing locations (see Table 1.1).

In his characterization of drug markets, Eck (1994) emphasizes ways that risk is managed. He argues that buyers and sellers both need to balance access to the market with security concerns. Too much access decreases security, whereas too much security on the part of one scares the other. Eck proposes two solutions to these problems, which define two market types. The first only connects individuals in a closed social network. Buying and selling occurs only among a limited number of network members or outsiders screened by a network member. These markets have low place attachment and can therefore tolerate spatial dislocation brought on by police crackdowns.

Eck's second type of market uses the geography of routine activities to bring together buyers and sellers who may be strangers to each other. In this model, dealers locate arterial routes and high-activity nodes where they must stay so that buyers can find them. The size of the market can grow much larger than a social network

TABLE 1.1 Buerger's Typology of Drug Markets

Type of Market	Distinguishing Features
Club	Sells only to known customers.
Speakeasy	Requires buyer to know password for admittance.
Drive-In	Buyer places order with intermediary, who obtains drugs and delivers them to buyer. Seller is protected.
Dealership	Intermediary takes orders and brings buyer to seller. Intermediary does not handle cash or drugs.
Bazaar	Large numbers of intermediaries work in public space making contacts with buyers and exchanging drugs for cash.
Cuckoo's Nest	Market operated out of abandoned building.
Rotation System	Market in continually changing locations.

SOURCE: Buerger (1992).

because transactions may be conducted with strangers. But high place attachment leaves such markets susceptible to law enforcement crackdowns.

Why Street-Level Antidrug Strategies Are Important

Traditional law enforcement work has been aimed at curbing the sale of illegal drugs by preventing them from entering the country or by disrupting organizations that control distribution. These strategies did not work well during the explosion of cocaine use in the late 1980s, however (Buerger, 1992). Despite a massive federal law enforcement effort and large numbers of arrests and convictions, the amount of cocaine on the streets increased, the price dropped, and the number of users increased sharply (Reuter & Haaga, 1989).

There are a number of reasons why high-level law enforcement efforts are relatively ineffective against cocaine sales. Enforcement efforts are usually intended to make the quantity of drugs scarce, which drives up retail prices. Research has suggested that federal enforcement activities that undermine foreign production, interdict imported drugs, or eliminate domestic producers are likely to have limited effects on drug sales. Because these sources have relatively little influence on the street value of illegal drugs, targeting them is likely to affect street prices only modestly (Reuter & Kleiman, 1986). Moreover, because the value of drugs seized early in the distribution chain is low and the cost of enforcement is high, the gains of these activities may not justify their cost (Kleiman, 1992).

Researchers have suggested that cocaine distribution networks are not "durable and hierarchical enterprises, but consist rather of temporary and shifting coalitions of dealers" (Reuter & Haaga, 1989, p. v). It has been suggested that barriers to entry into these markets are minimal, including neither long apprenticeship nor large amounts of cash. Thus, new organizations or individuals can easily replace those incapacitated by law enforcement efforts.

Law enforcement efforts directed against distribution networks may also have undesired consequences. Martens (1988) believes that enforcement can change the balance of power in markets with multiple suppliers, which may lead to monopolies or cartels that control the drug trade. If enforcement activities succeed in increasing the street prices of drugs, crime may increase as well. Brown and Silverman (1974) report a positive relationship between monthly heroin prices and crime in New York City. Higher prices appeared to induce addicts to commit more crimes to sustain their habits.

Neighborhood-Level
Enforcement of Drug Laws

Criminal Justice Approaches

Because of the serious problems associated with high-level drug enforcement activities, Kleiman suggests attacking drugs at the neighborhood level (Kleiman, 1992; Kleiman & Smith, 1990; Reuter & Kleiman, 1986). Proponents of neighborhood-level antidrug enforcement claim that such efforts can increase the nonmonetary costs of drugs and can reduce demand even though the price of the drugs will probably remain unchanged. For example, police drug sweeps or "buy-and-bust" operations force drug dealers to move to new locations or to become more discreet in their sales activities. Customers find it more difficult to locate suppliers and spend more time searching for drugs. Sweeps also increase the risk of arrest for both sellers and buyers. According to Kleiman (1992), "retail-level enforcement, which drug enforcement professionals often dismiss as making garbage cases, is more important than high-level, quality-case enforcement directed at drug kingpins, major money launderers, and other glamorous targets" (p. 9).

Neighborhood-level enforcement makes sense in light of the drug policy goals that Kleiman and Smith (1990) recommend: limiting the number of drug users, reducing drug-related crime, precluding the growth of stable and powerful drug organizations, and preventing the destructive neighborhood disorder that drug dealing causes. Kleiman and Smith maintain that a properly implemented neighborhood antidrug effort can facilitate each of these goals:

> It reduces drug abuse by reducing availability; it reduces user crime by reducing consumption without raising price; by the same token, it weakens major drug-dealing organizations by reducing the dollar value of the market; and it protects neighborhoods by reducing the flagrancy of illicit drug activity. (p. 86)

Kleiman and Smith (1990) also recognize that there are a number of potential problems when neighborhood-level enforcement is implemented through police sweeps. These problems are not trivial; they include the potential for displacement of drug sellers from one neighborhood to another and for police corruption and abuse of power. In addition, police sweeps are costly to run and may produce a deluge of arrestees that the courts are not equipped to handle.

Community policing is an alternative to the sweeps and mass arrests favored for controlling drug sales in traditional policing approaches. Community policing involves a variety of order-maintenance activities, for example, taking care of disorderly behaviors such as public drinking, prostitution, soliciting, and loitering (Wilson & Kelling, 1982). In the community policing model, order maintenance is seen as important because it directly reduces fear of crime and incivilities, which lead inexorably to further crime and neighborhood decline. Because drug activity is a particularly deleterious form of disorder, community policing demonstrates promise as an effective way to combat drug sales and use.

Community policing fosters close relationships between the police and community residents for enforcing norms about acceptable public behavior and promoting informal social control mechanisms in the community. These goals are accomplished through foot patrols and regular contact between police officials and community groups, which gives residents a chance to express their concerns and to influence police priorities. Community policing also involves broad approaches for combating disorder. The police serve as advocates for community residents in their dealings with building inspectors, sanitation officials, and staff of other city agencies. Some critics, however, have questioned several features of the disorder-decline model, which are central to community policing (e.g., Greene & Taylor, 1988).

Drug house abatement is another law enforcement response to neighborhood drug problems. This approach breaks new ground by drawing on civil rather than criminal procedures to force property owners to abate drug sales on their premises. Abatement programs are typically very inexpensive compared to arrests and other police efforts to reduce drug dealing.

Private Citizens' Initiatives

Action by law enforcement agencies is only one approach to fighting drugs at the neighborhood level. As we shall see, pure law enforcement approaches by themselves may have, at most, a minimal effect on drug sales in a community. Simply put, law enforcement authorities acknowledge that the police alone cannot carry out anticrime efforts at the community level. Criminal justice experts have noted that the best hope for curtailing drugs and crime in inner-city neighborhoods lies with the cooperation and involvement of local residents (Lavrakas, 1985; Rosenbaum, 1988). Citizen involvement in the fight to rid neighborhoods of drugs and crime is crucial.

The actions of residents in poor neighborhoods victimized by drugs was a surprising twist in the crack epidemic of the late 1980s. Residents of drug-plagued areas across the country initiated antidrug patrols, marches, and vigils; they have also implemented drug-reporting programs and instituted environmental changes to deny drug dealers a favorable setting for conducting their business. Most citizen initiatives have been undertaken in close cooperation with police enforcement efforts, but in places where officials have been slow to react to citizens' complaints of drugs or where citizens distrust the police, residents themselves have assumed responsibility for taking back their neighborhoods from drug dealers.

The story of residents in poor, inner-city neighborhoods fighting back against drugs is truly remarkable, because these neighborhoods largely had been written off by experts in community crime prevention. Neighbors banding together to fight crime is not a new phenomenon. Beginning in the 1970s, the federal government provided money and technical assistance to communities interested in citizen programs to reduce residential burglaries and street crimes. A great deal of research was undertaken on citizen anticrime efforts, including several large-scale experiments in which community organizers galvanized citizens in selected neighborhoods. This research, described in Chapter 3, generally showed that community anticrime programs were unlikely to take root in poor, high-crime neighborhoods—exactly those neighborhoods in which programs were most needed.

In the late 1980s, however, the residents of poor urban neighborhoods began to fight back against drugs on their streets. In response to the outbreak of disorder and violence associated with the sale of crack and other drugs, people began to join with their neighbors in concerted opposition to drugs and crime. The media featured various accounts of residents in inner-city neighborhoods joining together to combat drug dealers out of sheer anger and desperation. One of the earliest and best-publicized examples was in Washington, D.C. Drug dealers there had established an open-air drug market in a housing project called Mayfair Mansions. Crime and violence soared despite the efforts of the police. Nation of Islam members patrolling the area with walkie-talkies prevented crack dealers from gaining access to vacant apartments. They also started a drug treatment program. Aggressive confrontations with the dealers led to several acts of violence and to a tangible decline in drug sales. Residents were delighted. At first, the police were skeptical about the Nation of Islam efforts, but they later supported the activities ("Enter the Muslims," 1989; "Police Swarm," 1988).

Most of these citizen initiatives were spontaneous reactions to shootings or other violent acts stemming from drug dealing. Many were short lived and became dormant when residents grew weary or when drug dealers had been (at least temporarily) driven underground or out of the neighborhood. Nonetheless, some of these indigenous efforts persisted for years and grew in size and scope. Moreover, the media described these grassroots activists as being quite successful against neighborhood drug dealers. This success was not predicted by the evaluations of community programs to prevent street crimes and burglaries discussed in Chapter 3.

Of course, media accounts alone cannot provide a valid basis for drawing conclusions about the effectiveness of community antidrug programs. Journalists are more likely to report on unusual or successful initiatives and may have overstated the extent to which grassroots antidrug efforts have arisen in impoverished communities and had affected drug sales in those communities.

Fortunately, over the past several years, researchers have begun to rigorously investigate community antidrug programs. We report data indicating that the best grassroots antidrug initiatives are indeed successful in reducing neighborhood drug activity, fear of crime, and signs of social and physical disorder. This evidence has come both from case studies and surveys of residents in neighborhoods plagued by drugs and crime.

Although some citizen initiatives appear successful, that does not mean that all, or even most, are. And it is not clear how long they last. As citizen outrage fades and motivation diminishes, many initiatives languish and die. Citizen antidrug efforts can also cause unexpected problems. The drug dealer displaced from an activist neighborhood may simply move to a less antagonistic, adjacent neighborhood (Lab, 1992). From an urban policy perspective, the problem remains; it has just shifted geographically. Some observers have raised the specter of vigilantism in connection with citizen antidrug initiatives. Others have voiced concerns about infringements on civil liberties, which can occur as the result of police attempts to control drug trafficking (Rosenbaum, 1993).

A Conceptualization of
Neighborhood Antidrug Responses

Figure 1.3 depicts a continuum of antidrug enforcement efforts that can be launched at the local level. We have arrayed efforts according to degree of citizen involvement. Indigenous community antidrug initiatives are the purest example of citizens working on their own. Implanted community antidrug programs are next on the continuum: Government initiates them, supports them, and helps to organize them.

Drug abatement efforts—programs aimed at pressuring property owners to clean up drug nuisances under threat of civil action—are usually operated out of city attorneys' offices with close cooperation from police agencies. Such programs typically rely on citizen input through community meetings or "tip lines," identifying locations for abatement actions. Private citizens have invoked civil drug nuisance statutes to initiate and operate abatement programs exclusively.

Police efforts can be divided into traditional policing methods— undercover surveillance, buy-and-bust operations, reverse stings, and crackdowns—and community policing methods. Traditional police approaches to combat drugs often involve the use of inside informants but do not rely heavily on citizen participation. Community policing, on the other hand, commits police agencies to solicit the cooperation of citizens in defining problems and working toward solutions.

Other approaches to neighborhood drug enforcement (e.g., Cheh, 1991; Kleiman & Smith, 1990) are not discussed in this volume. These include asset forfeiture (where law enforcement officials seize property under federal and state laws) and code enforcement (where properties are cited with housing, fire, or health code violations to pressure owners to abate drug selling). Asset forfeiture is a powerful tool, but it is seldom worth the trouble in poor neighborhoods where

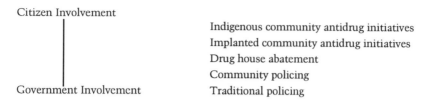

Figure 1.3. A Continuum of Neighborhood Responses to Drugs

houses are worth little. Code enforcement is usually a minor part of local strategies to curb local drug nuisances.

All of the strategies we discuss fit with recent perspectives on crime control based on the assumption that "crime can be controlled by changing situations and environmental factors so that individuals perceive potential targets less favorably" (Green, 1996, p. 18). Cornish and Clarke (1986) assume that offenders make rational choices about being involved in criminal behavior according to the expected gains and costs of committing crimes. For example, Reuter, MacCoun, and Murphy (1990) concluded that persons sell drugs because the money they earn by doing so exceeds the money they could earn through legitimate means.

Situational crime prevention perspectives build on the rational choice model by assuming that crime can be controlled by altering situations and environmental factors so that potential criminals perceive the potential costs to outweigh the expected gains (Clarke, 1992). Clarke divides crime control tactics into three categories: those that increase the effort to be involved in criminal activity, those that increase the risks to potential offenders, and those that decrease the expected gains from criminal activities.

Neighborhood antidrug strategies incorporate one or more of Clarke's (1992) three basic crime control tactics. Police crackdowns increase the effort required to buy or sell drugs by creating an environment in which it is more difficult (because the police temporarily "own" the streets) for buyers and sellers to come together to close a transaction. Citizen patrols or block watch programs increase neighborhood surveillance, thereby increasing drug sellers' risk of being caught. Asset forfeiture reduces the potential gains from drug sales.

Contents of This Volume

In this book, we discuss several types of neighborhood antidrug activities. In Chapter 2, we discuss a basic action that private citizens can take regarding drug activity in their neighborhoods—calling the police. We report data on people's willingness to call the police and the risks involved in choosing that alternative. We also discuss what the police do with citizen reports of drug activity. Are citizen reports useful to the police? Do they just clog up the 911 lines and detract from the ability of the police to handle violent crimes? We conclude with a case study of Philadelphia's South Division drug-reporting efforts.

In Chapter 3, we explore indigenous community antidrug programs. We discuss the various forms, from antidrug rallies to citizen patrols to educational interventions. We also describe the conditions necessary to implement community antidrug efforts, that is, the precipitating incidents that led to citizen responses; the critical role of strong program leaders; and the characteristics of communities that have instituted citizens' initiatives. In addition, we discuss data regarding the effects of these initiatives on residents' perceptions of drugs, crime, and disorder. We return to Philadelphia's South Division to present a case study of a successful, indigenous antidrug program known as Let's Clean It Up (LCIU).

In Chapter 4, we examine the topic of implanted community antidrug programs. In contrast to indigenous efforts, implanted programs are established with external funds and are organized from outside the community. With implanted antidrug programs, it is possible to use more rigorous research designs to evaluate the effectiveness of citizen antidrug activities. Findings about implanted programs may not necessarily apply to indigenous programs, however. We discuss four major undertakings: Community Responses to Drug Abuse Program, Community Partnership Program, Fighting Back, and Weed and Seed. Chapter 4 concludes with a description of the Hartford, Connecticut, Areas Rally Together (HART) Program, a coalition of neighborhood organizations engaged in a variety of activities to combat drugs and rebuild communities.

Chapter 5 deals with police efforts to combat illegal drugs. We discuss traditional law enforcement approaches, their impact on drug dealers, and their strengths and weaknesses as strategies to combat drugs. We also discuss community policing, a problem-oriented approach to controlling drugs and other signs of disorder in poor neighborhoods. Our case study in Chapter 5 is focused on another program in Hartford called the Cartographic Oriented Management Program for the Abatement of Street Sales (COMPASS), in which drug market analysis and the "weed and seed" model are employed to rid neighborhoods of drug businesses and activities.

In Chapter 6, we examine another law enforcement approach to drugs that seems remarkably cost-effective—drug house abatement programs. These programs target owners of properties where drugs are being sold. Owners are forced to abate drug nuisances under threat of civil penalties, which may include fines or forfeiture of property. Like other law enforcement strategies for fighting drugs, abatement programs raise questions about the violation of citizens' rights and the displacement of illegal activity to surrounding neighborhoods. At the end of Chapter 6, we discuss Milwaukee's successful Drug Abatement Team and examine the downside of drug abatement efforts.

In the final chapter, we summarize what is known about neighborhood approaches to combating illegal drugs. We place research findings in the context of theories about drug transactions and community crime prevention. To conclude, we discuss the implications of neighborhood antidrug efforts for the future of community crime prevention programs.

2. Citizen Reporting of Drug Activity

Reporting information to the police is the most basic response citizens can make to unwanted drug activity in their neighborhoods. Do the violent and intimidating methods of some drug dealers dissuade citizens from calling? What risks do people incur by calling the police? How do the police respond to complaints about drug activity? Do citizens' reports help police to target drug sales? What attention do the police give to drug complaints compared to murders, robberies, rapes, and other violent crimes? In this chapter, we examine these questions about citizens' drug-related complaints.

First, we briefly review the literature on victim and bystander reporting of crimes and discuss what this literature suggests about people's willingness to report drug activity. Second, we summarize data on the question of how willing people are to report drug activity relative to violent and property crimes. We examine the willingness of residents in different neighborhoods to report drug activity and explain differences between neighborhoods by discussing residents' perceptions about their communities. Third, we focus on how the police process citizens' drug complaints and whether those complaints are useful to the police in their efforts against drug dealers. Finally, we explore new techniques law enforcement officials use to encourage citizen reporting of drug activity and to increase the usefulness of those reports in solving drug crimes. The chapter concludes with a case study.

Citizens' Willingness to Report Crime

Over the past two decades, researchers have studied victims' willingness to report crimes and bystanders' willingness to intervene in criminal events. Neither of these types of studies deals directly with drug activity, however. In contrast to the incidents examined in the literature on victim reporting, drug activity is a so-called victimless or consensual crime. Research on victim reporting involves people who have experienced the material, medical, or psychological costs associated with being crime victims. Their stake in reporting is arguably greater than that of persons who live in neighborhoods that are being victimized by drug activity.

Skogan (1988), Wilson and Kelling (1982), and others consider drug activity an indicator of neighborhood "incivility," along with graffiti, trash in the street, and gangs of teens hanging out on corners. These phenomena are distinct from crime. People exposed to local drug activity fall somewhere between victims and bystanders in the customary senses of these terms.

Although people who witness drug activity in their neighborhoods are not exactly victims or bystanders, prior research does suggest why they may (or may not) be willing to report drug activity. The literature on victim reporting indicates that the greater the immediate costs of crime to victims, as measured by financial loss or physical injury, the greater the likelihood that they will report their victimization (e.g., Gottfredson & Hindelang, 1979; Waller & Okihiro, 1978). A major reason for not reporting crime is the victim's belief that authorities can do little to help in the incident (Schneider, Burcart, & Wilson, 1976; U.S. Department of Justice, 1981). In most cases of this kind, the individuals are victimized by crimes that actually have a minimal likelihood of being solved (Skogan & Antunes, 1979; Sparks, Genn, & Dodd, 1977).

The bystander intervention literature is consistent with the victim reporting literature. Studies in this field show that people are more likely to take action when they perceive a situation to be clearly serious (Piliavin, Doridio, Gaertner, & Clark, 1981). Research also suggests that people are less likely to intervene in a criminal incident when other witnesses are around (Bickman & Rosenbaum, 1977; Latane & Darley, 1969). Furthermore, when the costs of intervention are perceived as high (e.g., in situations where people fear retaliation), people are less likely to intervene than when the costs are perceived as low (Piliavin et al., 1981; Rosenbaum, Lurigio, & Lavrakas, 1989).

What do these studies suggest about citizens reporting drug activity? Most of the factors that contribute to citizens' inaction with regard to other crimes also seem to militate against the reporting of drug activity. Drug activity is a victimless crime. Neighborhood residents do not normally sustain injuries or property loss. Authorities may be perceived as ineffective in alleviating the problem because it is sometimes difficult to catch drug dealers or users in the act or because courts and correctional facilities seem to make few inroads against drug and violent crime cases. People may perceive the costs of intervention as high because of drug dealers' threats or extensive media coverage of the violence perpetrated against and by drug dealers. Finally, people may feel little personal responsibility to report drug crimes because other residents also have knowledge of the problem.

Media accounts tend to reinforce the idea that residents of poor urban neighborhoods, where drug activity thrives, are afraid to report drug sales to authorities or have been dissuaded by financial incentives or familial ties with drug traffickers (e.g., "Murder Zones," 1989; "Some Residents," 1989). Police freely admit that threats against residents who interfere with the drug trade are common, but they also note that retaliation is the exception rather than the rule. Still, it is not unheard of for witnesses to be murdered after they report drug activity or testify against drug dealers ("Threats of Death," 1989). A single such incident can have a chilling effect on an entire community.

Data on Citizens' Drug Reporting

The data that we present come from an American Bar Association (ABA) study funded by the National Institute of Justice (Davis, Smith, & Hillenbrand, 1991). The researchers examined citizen reporting behavior through resident surveys and on-site interviews with police in two neighborhoods in each of four cities: Chicago, Illinois; Newark, New Jersey; Philadelphia, Pennsylvania; and El Paso, Texas. In each neighborhood, researchers interviewed approximately 50 citizens. In addition, the researchers conducted a national telephone survey with police chiefs or their designates in 46 of the 50 largest U.S. cities. Interviewers elicited respondents' opinions on whether citizen reports were useful to the police.

All eight neighborhoods had serious drug problems. When respondents were asked to rate a list of nine potential neighborhood problems (including crime, gangs, vacant buildings, and abandoned cars), they ranked drugs Number 1. Although all the neighborhoods were poor, they varied significantly in degree of resident transience, neighborhood cohesion, and resident satisfaction with the neighborhood.

The investigators in the ABA study were concerned about losing respondents if they immediately asked them about their personal reporting of drug activity. They attempted to ease respondents into discussions of their own experiences by first asking them about the general behavior of people in their neighborhoods. The results showed that just one in five respondents indicated that "most" residents in their communities reported drug sales or use when they saw it. Another one in five responded that "some" residents reported drug sales or use. In sharp contrast, more than three in five residents said that "most" people in their neighborhoods reported crimes other than drug activity. Relative to other types of crime, then, drug sales and use were grossly underreported.

Responses to specific questions about interviewees' own reporting behavior confirmed the finding that drug activity was underreported. Although the vast majority of residents acknowledged that they had witnessed drug activity in their neighborhoods, only one in seven said that they had ever reported it to the police. Table 2.1

TABLE 2.1 Frequency of People Witnessing and Reporting Various
Forms of Drug Activity

	Percentage Who Have Seen Activity	Percentage of Those Reporting Activity Who Saw It
People taking drugs on streets (N = 175)	45	19
People taking drugs in buildings (N = 109)	27	10
People entering shooting galleries (N = 57)	14	18
Kids buying/selling drugs (N = 81)	21	20
People selling drugs on streets (N = 201)	50	22
People selling drugs around schools (N = 73)	15	20
People selling drugs from homes (N = 111)	23	23
People delivering/moving quantities of drugs (N = 37)	8	28

SOURCE: Davis, Smith, and Hillenbrand (1991).

shows that the most commonly witnessed drug activities were people selling or taking drugs on the street; roughly half of the respondents reported viewing each of those activities. Table 2.1 also shows that the activities most likely to be reported (when witnessed) were deliveries of drugs and sales of drugs from homes. Only one in five respondents who witnessed these activities reported them to the police.

Both residents and police respondents from each district were asked to rate a series of reasons that might make people reluctant to report drug activity. Residents' and officers' rank orderings of the reasons were highly consistent (see Table 2.2). Fear of revenge was at the top of both lists. Although the resident survey uncovered few incidents of actual retaliation, one in nine respondents who reported drug activity was threatened with violence as a result.

The next most common reason for not reporting drug activity was reluctance to go to court and testify. When asked later in the survey about what would make them more willing to report drug-related information, the most popular response was "guaranteed anonymity" if they called in a complaint. Again, respondents were indicating that they were scared and probably reluctant to volunteer large

TABLE 2.2 Percentage Distribution of Citizen and Patrol Officer Responses to What Stops People From Reporting Drug Activity

Item	Patrol Officers (N = 33)	Residents (N = 402)
Fear of revenge	45 (1)	76 (1)
Worry about going to court and testifying	42 (2)	67 (2)
Worry that reporting could get them into trouble with police	34 (3)	39 (4)
Belief that reporting is a waste of time	32 (4)	49 (3)
Belief that drugs do not hurt community	8 (8)	9 (8)
Belief that police are already aware of drug activity observed	27 (5)	24 (6.5)
Belief that drugs help community economy	2 (9)	6 (9)
Belief that drug activity is none of their business	17 (7)	33 (5)

SOURCE: Davis, Smith, and Hillenbrand (1991).
NOTE: Figures in parentheses are rank orderings of each item. Figures are percentages of those who responded "often" to each item. Spearman's rho = .95 between resident and police officer responses.

amounts of their time cooperating with the police. The next two items on the resident and police lists were a belief that reporting would just be a waste of time and worry that reporting would get residents in trouble with authorities. Both of these reasons seem to underscore the distrust that neighborhood residents have of police.

Substantial differences were found among the eight neighborhoods with respect to residents' willingness to report drug activity. In El Paso's Central Police District and Chicago's Seventh Police District, for example, only 9% and 12% of the respondents, respectively, stated that "most" people in their neighborhood reported drug activity. In sharp contrast, 51% of respondents in Newark's West Police District and 31% of respondents in El Paso's East Valley Police District stated that most people reported drug activity.

The ABA researchers identified two factors that differentiated communities in which residents were willing to report drug activity from those in which residents were not. The first factor, community viability, was defined by residents' perceptions of the extensiveness of drug activity and other community problems, the quality of municipal services, police-community relations, and social cohesion. The second factor, socioeconomic status, was defined by education and income. These two factors were independent— among the communities in the study, researchers found no relationship between socioeconomic status and community health or viability.

Both these factors explained the reporting of drug activity, but community viability was, by far, the better predictor, explaining nearly 25% of all of the differences in reporting behavior compared to just 5% for socioeconomic status. The investigators concluded that, "Willingness to report is less in places where municipal services, police-community relations, and social ties between neighbors have deteriorated. Unfortunately, these are also the districts which tend to have the worst problems with drugs" (Davis, Smith, & Hillenbrand, 1991, p. 87).

How the Police Process Drug Complaints

A basic question concerning citizen complaints about drug activity is how much do the police rely on such reports? Law enforcement data indicate that police in major cities are overwhelmed with citizen reports of drug activity; they simply receive many more reports of drug activity than they can ever effectively handle.

Channels of Reporting. Drug activity can be reported to police through a number of different channels. Most citizens' reports come through 911 calls to a central dispatcher of patrol units. When response time is quick, calls to 911 may result in police catching a drug dealer in action. Unfortunately, that seldom happens, because complaints of drug activity are given low priority relative to homicides, robberies, and other violent crimes. On a Friday or Saturday night, several hours may pass before a police department dispatches a patrol car to answer a drug complaint. In fact, some police contend that the drug complaints are an inappropriate use of 911 systems, which ought to be reserved for true emergencies. Another problem with 911 reports is keeping the callers' identities anonymous. Drug dealers sometimes monitor police radio communications, and in some states, 911 calls are available to the media or anyone else who requests access to them.

Citizens who want to report drug activity can also directly call their police department's central narcotics unit or make indirect contact through special drug hotlines. Central reporting systems typically maintain high levels of accountability, ensuring that reports do not get lost in the shuffle and that citizens who report information can call back later to find out how the police responded to their call. Calling a central narcotics unit makes sense for persons who are reporting major drug-dealing operations or stashes of large quantities of drugs. These are the kinds of cases—high profile and involving several districts—that narcotics detectives like to tackle. For the typical cases that narcotics detectives handle, however, they rely more on reports from a few informants with inside knowledge about the drug trade than on reports from concerned citizens.

Most information that citizens have to report is information on low-level retail drug outlets (Sherman, 1992) and is not of consequence to the cases against distribution networks that central narcotics units are likely to pursue. The bulk of complaints made by ordinary citizens to central narcotics units are passed along to district commanders. Several days are likely to pass, and because the reports are usually anonymous, district commanders have no way to refresh the outdated information.

Some people call their local police district, which may entail security risks to callers if officers have been bought off by local drug dealers. (Although corruption is not a common occurrence, police administrators in several of the districts visited in the ABA study expressed this concern.) Conversely, calling a local district with information about drugs may foster an ongoing relationship between the caller and district officers.

Are Citizens' Reports Useful? The majority of citizens' complaints about drugs provide the police with little new information. Citizens' calls are often redundant with earlier calls from other residents, with information from informants, or with intelligence from police officers on patrol or stakeout. Citizens often provide little specific information on a dealer's identity or the location of a dealer's drugs or supply sources. One captain in Newark was quoted in the ABA study as saying that the police "know exactly where drugs are sold throughout the city. Of the reports of locations we get, we already know about 99% of them" (Davis, Smith, & Hillenbrand, 1991, p. 60).

Despite their limitations, citizens' reports are useful to the police to identify drug "hot spots" and allocate resources to areas of heavy drug trafficking. Citizens' calls are seen as most useful at the district level, where commanders are concerned about responding to community needs. In districts where drugs are ubiquitous, residents' complaints alert commanders to those neighborhoods in which people are willing to do something about the problem. The ABA study found that district commanders welcomed community groups' efforts to organize residents to surveil their neighborhoods and to report drug activity. The commanders responded by giving those neighborhoods whatever help they needed in the form of undercover surveillance, uniformed patrols, pressure on property owners to evict sellers, and assistance in organizing antidrug rallies.

In contrast to general complaints about drug sales, specific reports containing detailed information—especially about the sale or distribution of drugs from indoor locations—are highly useful to the police (Sherman, 1992). These reports may supply information about locations or individuals that can be used to obtain search warrants or justify undercover surveillance or drug buys. Such reports are typically acted on by central narcotics units (or, less commonly, by district-level tactical units), which have the staff, equipment, and intelligence network needed to confirm the reports and to take appropriate action.

Ways to Develop Better Reporting Systems. The ABA study recommended that police departments develop new ways to process citizens' complaints about drugs, which, by themselves, generally have little value to anyone at headquarters. Nevertheless, a pattern of calls in a district is informative to district commanders because it alerts them to areas of unusually high drug activity or resident concern about drug activity. Therefore, departments are well advised to direct these reports to the local districts, either by switching over live 911 calls or by routing the call slips that the 911 operators prepare.

As these results are fed into local districts, the information can be collated to detect patterns of drug activity emanating from particular locations within the district (see, e.g., the work of Sherman, Gartin, & Buerger, 1989, on the utility of focusing police resources on crime hot spots). The most efficient way to do this is with a computer, which could also merge reports of drug activity with information about other criminal activity at specified locations. The ABA researchers noted that some departments were beginning to develop such systems. (Since that time, the National Institute of Justice Drug Market Analysis Program—DMAP—has developed such systems in five cities; see Taxman & McEwen, 1994; Weisburd & Green, 1994. DMAP is described in detail in Chapter 5.) By using a computer data base to record patterns of drug activity, departments now have the ability to act preemptively against drug trafficking. Without such collective data, they can only react by dispatching patrol units to respond to each separate call. Once a pattern is detected, the police can interview residents, set up a surveillance capacity, and conduct buy-and-bust operations.

For such a system to work, the police have to lower callers' expectations that a patrol car will be dispatched promptly to respond to their particular reports. (This is essentially the position reached by Spelman & Brown, 1984, who found that prompt dispatch of patrol units did little to increase the odds of apprehending criminals.) The police need to tell callers that their reports will be used to produce an overall picture of criminal activity in the area, which the police will watch closely and act on using appropriate means. This kind of honesty might actually improve police-community relations, which are damaged when callers expect swift action but receive only a long-delayed response or no response at all.

The ABA study also suggests that the police explore ways to improve the quality of citizens' reports. The investigators found such efforts in New York City and Philadelphia. In Philadelphia, local police administrators were training members of community groups to report specific information about drug dealing, including the identities of the individuals involved, their methods of operation, and the locations of their drugs. A small group of these citizens was given access to police radios so they could directly report nonemergency activities to local district officers. This direct channel gave responding officers an opportunity to request follow-up information from callers and increased the chances that the police would arrive at the scene in time to apprehend suspects and to seize evidence. The ABA report recommends that police departments using this approach formulate strict guidelines governing citizen behavior and explaining the liability that the department would assume for citizens killed, injured, or sued in the course of these activities.

The ABA researchers also concluded that police departments should protect the anonymity of callers who do not wish their identities disclosed. They recommended procedural changes such as withholding complainants' names and addresses over police radios and instructing responding officers to go to complainants' homes only when callers have granted them permission to do so. Finally, they suggested that mechanisms be instituted to give citizens information on the actions taken as a result of their calls.

New Reporting Modalities

Recently, new methods of reporting drug activity have appeared in cities across the country; these methods protect caller anonymity and provide information to citizens on police responses to calls. For example, Crime Stoppers is a network of privately run hotlines for reporting crime tips. Although its operation predates the recent crack epidemic, many of the calls that Crime Stoppers receives are now drug related. Financial rewards are given to callers when their information results in an arrest or conviction. The amount of the reward depends on the quantity of drugs seized in arrests. To protect their anonymity, callers are assigned a number that identifies them at follow-up. Repeat calls by the same person are common, and such individuals may become quite adept at ascertaining and reporting the type of information police find useful (Rosenbaum et al., 1989).

Many police departments have implemented special drug hotlines that route complaints either to a central narcotics unit or to district officers. These hotlines offer callers anonymity, but may be staffed only during certain hours of the day. The New York City police developed an innovative variation to this approach. Their Drug Busters Program enlists residents to surveil their neighborhood and to report drug activity to a special hotline. After police officers train residents on how to collect drug-related information, they assign to each of them an identification number to be used when calling in a complaint. Callers then use those numbers to find out what actions police took in response to their complaints.

Finally, some community groups field complaints from neighborhood residents and pass that information along to police officers in the local district. This reporting strategy is designed to elicit complaints from residents who do not want to report directly to the police for any number of reasons: They may be hostile to the police, they may be criminally involved, they may not trust the police to keep their reports confidential, or they may fear being asked to testify in court. For example, residents of Boston's Roxbury area can report drug activity to Drop-a-Dime, an antidrug program that records complaints anonymously on a 24-hour message machine (National Center for Neighborhood Enterprise, 1990). Program staff relate these messages to the police who inform program members on the actions taken in response to their calls. On a larger scale, Milwaukee's Cooperation West Side Association (COWSA) receives anonymous drug complaints and tracks patterns of drug trafficking. Periodically, COWSA staff fax data on current hot spots to police detectives. The police report to COWSA any action taken against problem locations (Smith, Davis, Hillenbrand, & Goretsky, 1992).

Profile of a Successful Program:
The Philadelphia Police Department
Response to Drug Reports

In Philadelphia, the police department's handling of drug reports in the city's South Division is multifaceted. South Division covers 13 square miles of inner-city neighborhoods with a quarter of a million residents. The division has four districts staffed by 600 sworn officers. The police encourage citizens to report drug crimes and to surveil their neighborhoods for drug activity. The police response to drug reports in South Division consists of a range of options, from immediately dispatching uniformed officers, to deploying low-level undercover officers to conduct surveillance, to commanding the centralized narcotics unit to launch a major investigation. The police track activity at drug hot spots through a computer, and they attempt to clean up problem locations before drug problems can escalate.

South Division was a national leader in adopting community- and problem-oriented policing practices. In 1988, the police department established a ministation in Queens Village, a 6-square-block neighborhood in South Division, which includes a thriving retail section, an artisan community, a large public housing complex, and private residences. Shortly thereafter, the department opened a second ministation in the Martin Luther King neighborhood.

The two ministations serve socioeconomically and ethnically diverse neighborhoods with serious crime and drug problems. In both neighborhoods, the police work closely with an advisory committee composed of local residents, business and religious leaders, and representatives from private and city agencies. The committee defines community problems and attempts to solve them by deploying available resources.

The South Division police have developed a well-organized network of community antidrug initiatives, encouraging citizens to report drug activity directly to the police or to community leaders, who pass the information along to the police. The police have also mobilized a cadre of concerned citizens to act as the eyes and ears of law enforcement in drug hot spots. These citizens receive special training on what to look for (especially production, storage, and distribution centers) and what to report to the police to facilitate arrests. They are typically older, retired residents who are at home much of the day and have the time to surveil their neighborhood. They communicate with district field units via two-way police radio. When these citizens report drug sales in progress, their information is relayed immediately to patrol cars, making it possible for the police to actually catch drug dealers red-handed. After a patrol car responds, the citizen may relay additional information about any fleeing suspects.

Ordinary citizens may report drug activity to centralized numbers or to the local police district. Centralized numbers include calls to 911, which result in the dispatch of a patrol unit; calls to the police narcotics unit drug hotline; and calls to a Crime Stoppers hotline, which logs more than 1,000 calls annually. In either of the latter two cases, information that is not likely to lead to major cases is referred back to local districts. At the local district, reports usually result in the dispatch of patrol units to surveil the problem area. If a patrol confirms a report, the police may assign the case to an undercover unit for closer surveillance and a possible buy-and-bust operation.

The police log all drug-related calls that come into the South Division, regardless of source. They complete a form containing the address of the alleged activity, suspect names (if available), and other relevant information. If an arrest is made, they add it the incident data. The police input these incident reports into a computer that tracks drug sales and other illegal activities at addresses throughout the South Division. The computer produces reports that identify drug hot spots, and division field staff or members of the central narcotics unit are then dispatched to investigate these locations.

3. Community Antidrug Efforts

The Origins of Community Antidrug Efforts in the 1970s Community Anticrime Movement

Community antidrug efforts of the 1980s and 1990s grew out of citizen programs, which were started in the 1970s to prevent street crime and residential burglary. The fundamental philosophy of the community crime prevention movement was that the most effective means of combating crime is to involve residents in proactive interventions aimed at reducing or precluding the opportunity for crime in their neighborhoods (Lockhard, Duncan, & Brenner, 1978; Podolefsky & DuBow, 1981). Citizen programs to combat street crime and burglaries assumed a variety of forms, including resident patrols (Yin, Vogel, & Chaiken, 1977), citizen crime-reporting networks (Bickman, Lavrakas, & Green, 1977), block watch programs (Rosenbaum, Lewis, & Grant, 1985), home security surveys (International Training, Research, and Evaluation Council, 1977), property-marking projects (Heller, Stenzel, & Gill, 1975), police-community councils (Yin, 1979), and a variety of plans for changing the physical environment (e.g., Fowler & Mangione, 1986; Lavrakas & Kushmuk, 1986).

Community crime prevention is grounded in two basic theoretical models. The first model involves informal social control. This model suggests that reductions in crime and the fear of crime are by-products of various processes that include vigorous enforcement of social norms (Greenberg, Rohe, & Williams, 1982; Jacobs, 1961), clearer delineation of neighborhood boundaries and identities (Suttles, 1972), and establishment of a stronger sense of community and increased social interaction (Conklin, 1975; DuBow & Emmons, 1981). This model reflects what Podolefsky and DuBow (1981) describe as a social problem approach to community crime prevention, with efforts to reduce crime through the amelioration of the social conditions that breed criminal activity.

Community crime prevention projects are also rooted in an opportunity reduction model of crime prevention, emphasizing the deterrence value of designing or modifying the physical environment to enhance the security of commercial and residential settings (Heinzelmann, 1981, 1983) and encouraging residents to adopt measures to minimize their vulnerability to crime (Lavrakas, 1981; Lavrakas & Lewis, 1980). The latter is often achieved through formal, anticrime educational campaigns sponsored by the media, law enforcement officials, and citizen groups. In addition, opportunity reduction may involve fostering a closer relationship between local police and citizens by restructuring the deployment of patrol officers to increase their contact with community residents.

The theoretical approaches to community anticrime prevention were rooted in empirical studies of neighborhoods. Research demonstrated that high levels of social interaction among area residents are correlated with the enhancement of informal social control (Fischer, Jackson, Steuve, Gerson, & Jones, 1977). Other studies suggest that crime is lower in neighborhoods in which social control is higher, as indicated by residents' sense of responsibility for the area (Taylor, Gottfredson, & Brower, 1981), by their willingness to intervene in criminal acts (Maccoby, Johnson, & Church, 1958), and by their belief that their neighbors are willing to intervene to fight crime or prevent victimization (Newman & Franck, 1980).

In spite of the plausibility of the theoretical models and support-
ing data from correlational studies, the results of evaluations of
community anticrime programs were, at best, mixed. Most significant, community anticrime programs did not seem to take hold in
low income, high-crime neighborhoods where they were most needed.
Researchers found that naturally occurring or indigenous citizen
programs to combat burglary and robbery were more likely to be
started and sustained in relatively crime-free and orderly communities where residents are middle income and well educated and
own their own homes (Garofalo & McLeod, 1988; Greenberg et al.,
1982; Henig, 1982; Lavrakas & Lewis, 1980; Skogan, 1989; Skogan
& Maxfield, 1981).

Rosenbaum (1987) argues that the most reliable data on community crime prevention programs come from experiments that examine whether programs can be implanted in neighborhoods that do
not already have them. Such experiments were conducted in Chicago; Minneapolis; and Portland, Oregon. Results showed that even
when vigorous attempts are made to recruit area residents to join
neighborhood anticrime groups, overall participation levels are
low—ranging from 10% of households in Portland (Schneider, 1986)
to 16% in Chicago (Rosenbaum, Lewis, & Grant, 1986) to 18% in
Minneapolis (Pati, McPherson, & Silloway, 1987). Participation in
neighborhood anticrime groups was concentrated in communities
with affluent home-owning residents—communities that had the
fewest crime problems. Organizing was much less successful in
communities with poor, non-home-owning residents. This was true
even though far more organizing attempts were made in the less-
affluent neighborhoods of Minneapolis (Skogan, 1990). In a comprehensive review of the crime prevention literature, Rosenbaum
(1988) stated that,

> A major lesson from these experimental programs is that organizing
> and sustaining community interest in activities directed at reducing
> opportunity and creating informal social controls are considerably more
> difficult in low-income, heterogeneous areas that are most in need of
> crime prevention assistance. (p. 363)

Furthermore, most organizing efforts had few effects on the
development of informal social control in targeted neighborhoods,

as measured by social interaction, surveillance, crime reporting, and social cohesion. Experts in community crime prevention began to despair about organizing crime prevention programs in poor, inner-city communities. Greenberg et al. (1982) concluded that "studies simply do not demonstrate with any reasonable level of confidence that informal social control, in and of itself, affects crime" (p. 100). Rosenbaum (1987) contended that the entire concept of neighborhood watch is flawed. He argued further that little evidence exists that such programs change people's willingness to engage in social interaction, informal social control, or surveillance of the neighborhood. In addition, he maintained that even if these developments appeared as a result of the program, the changes would not be sufficient enough to affect local crime rates.

The Development of Community
Antidrug Programs in the Late 1980s and 1990s

Concern in the mid-1980s about the influx of crack cocaine and accompanying crime and disorder induced neighbors to band together to form anticrime programs directed against drug sellers. Many of these community antidrug programs have received a good deal of media coverage. According to the newspaper accounts, community antidrug initiatives are mostly found in the worst drug-infested neighborhoods. The *New York Times* has highlighted a number of antidrug efforts in Brooklyn's notorious Bedford-Stuyvesant district (Holmes, 1989; Morgan, 1988). Journalists have described citizen responses to drug activity in public housing developments in Cleveland, Fort Lauderdale, New York, and elsewhere (e.g., "Murder Zones," 1989). Poverty and social disorganization characterize these neighborhoods; they are just the sort of places in which citizens have been considered unlikely to initiate or sustain anticrime efforts.

The most surprising revelation in media accounts is that citizen initiatives, often minimally organized and unfinanced, have been highly successful in shutting down or severely curtailing local drug markets. Local newspapers reported that 100 residents of Houston's Acres Homes neighborhood united to chase drug dealers away from

a community park. The group then established an aggressive neighborhood watch program, which former President Bush praised on a
visit to Houston (Gerstenzang & Jehl, 1989; Gravois & Lanterman,
1989; Phillips, 1989).

Are the impressions given by the media accurate? Are poor,
inner-city residents fighting drugs and crime in ways that they have
not done in the past? Can these efforts truly make a difference? We
address these questions in this chapter and discuss data from the
first empirical attempts to examine the success of indigenous
anticrime initiatives. We conclude the chapter with an illustrative
case study.

Community Antidrug Initiatives

Community antidrug efforts come in all shapes and sizes. Some
are large and based on significant planning whereas others are small
and arise spontaneously. Many communities have pursued a law
enforcement approach to curbing drug sales; others have created alternatives for youth at risk of becoming involved in the drug trade. Many
work closely with local police and elected officials, but others are
openly hostile toward established authorities, which they view as
ineffective or uninterested in the problems of poor neighborhoods.

In a series of case studies on community antidrug initiatives,
Weingart, Hartmann, and Osborne (1992) broadly defined community antidrug efforts as "collection[s] of individuals who joined
together to participate in an activity oriented against drugs" (p. 5).
We use a similar definition here, with the stipulation that program
participants must have engaged in a sustained activity against
drugs. Our definition excludes onetime antidrug vigils or rallies that
do not lead to further action. For example, in 1990, church activists
organized vigils in several drug-infested neighborhoods in Trenton,
New Jersey. Although the vigils energized many people to demonstrate their opposition to neighborhood drug sales, they did not
produce a continuing crusade by local residents. We later describe
examples of successful grassroots efforts that stopped operating
once the participants had eradicated blatant drug selling in their
neighborhoods.

Varieties of Community
Antidrug Initiatives

Roehl, Wong, Huitt, and Capowich (1995) recently completed a nationwide study of community antidrug initiatives. To identify programs, they sought nominations from law enforcement agencies, the Center for Substance Abuse Prevention Community Partnership Programs' 251 grantees, the 15 Fighting Back programs sponsored by the Robert Wood Johnson Foundation, and the 10 sites in the Bureau of Justice Assistance Innovative Neighborhood Policing Program. This selection method probably biased the sample in favor of more "mainstream" initiatives. Nonetheless, the study is a systematic attempt to identify and describe community antidrug efforts.

Roehl et al. (1995) found that community antidrug initiatives were most prevalent in low-income urban neighborhoods where substance abuse, drug dealing, and social disorder are common. Most initiatives were relatively new. More than half had been established since 1985 and targeted entire cities.

The researchers identified several program types: loosely organized groups of citizens, block or neighborhood watch groups, grassroots groups, umbrella organizations, civic and service groups, church and religious groups, and "other." Grassroots groups were the most common program type, accounting for more than one in three initiatives in the sample. Umbrella organizations had the largest membership and budgets, whereas loosely organized citizens' groups and neighborhood watch groups had the least funding. In general, community antidrug programs had few paid staff and little external funding and one in three had no paid staff or external funding. The most common source of support came from local fund-raising efforts and individual contributions.

Roehl et al. (1995) also found that citizen involvement in the community antidrug initiatives generally was not high. Half of the programs they surveyed reported that fewer than 10% of community residents took part in the activities. Moreover, although many citizens participated in occasional marches or rallies, the programs reported that the vast majority did not become seriously involved in program activities due to apathy, denial, tolerance of drug use,

practical problems, or fear. Typically, most of the work was performed by small cadres of dedicated volunteers.

How Community Initiatives
Fight Against Drugs

What do community antidrug initiatives do to curb local drug
sales? Weingart (1993) suggests a typology of community responses
against drugs, based on program strategies. The first broad approach
to fighting drugs involves *law enforcement enhancement efforts*,
which are probably the most common way citizens fight against
drugs. Block watch groups, which exemplify this approach, have
existed in many neighborhoods throughout the country for more
than a decade (Rosenbaum, 1986). Recent concern about drugs has
revitalized existing groups and encouraged the formation of new
groups. As an illustration of the former, block watch participants
have learned to observe drug sales from their homes and to record
details of drug transactions, including descriptions of the participants and their vehicles and the locations of drug stashes. Some
groups report this information directly to the police, either to their
local station house or to a centralized narcotics hotline. For example, as we described in Chapter 2, the police in Philadelphia's South
Division trained a group of residents and equipped them with radios
so that patrol cars could be dispatched immediately to the scene of
a drug transaction before the drug dealers had a chance to slip away.

Block watch groups in neighborhoods where citizens distrust the
police report information to citizen-run hotlines. In Boston's notorious Roxbury neighborhood, a feisty grandmother started the Drop-
a-Dime Program out of her basement. The program gives residents
an opportunity to report drug activity anonymously to a 24-hour
message machine. Police value the program because it allows them
to observe patterns of complaints, which help them to plan broader
and more effective operations against drugs. A more traditional
method is to dispatch a patrol car in response to each complaint,
which is usually an ineffective strategy (see Chapter 2).

Citizen patrol is another type of activity that falls under the rubric
of law enforcement. Like block watch programs, citizen patrols
predate the drug crisis of the 1980s. Both media accounts and

evidence we review in this chapter suggest that recent citizen patrols can be a more potent weapon against drugs than their predecessors ever were against burglaries, robberies, and other street crimes in the 1970s. Today's citizen antidrug patrols confront specific individuals in the act of dealing drugs. Many programs have pursued aggressive patrol tactics that carry some risk of violence. The participants of New York City's Blockos Program simply stood near dealers and disrupted their business. The dealers eventually gave up and went away (Powers, 1993). Citizen patrols in Seattle's Ranier Valley and the Washington, D.C., Fairlawn section took pictures of dealers and tried to discourage their clients (Davis, Smith, Lurigio, & Skogan, 1991; Weingart, 1993). An extremely confrontational tactic was used in the early days of community activist Herman Wrice's Philadelphia Antidrug Coalition: Participants wielded sledgehammers to raid and board up crack houses (Lundberg, 1990).

Aggressive patrol tactics appear to be one of the most effective kinds of citizen responses to drug sales, but they clearly have the potential for provoking violent reactions from drug dealers. In 1988, members of the Nation of Islam patrolled the Mayfair Mansions apartment complex in Washington, D.C., carrying walkie-talkies and nightsticks and confronting drug dealers. Fights erupted between members and dealers but the situation quieted down after the first few days (Davis, 1989). Because of the risk of violence, the police usually discourage aggressive citizen patrol tactics. Police have lent grudging support to these efforts when citizen groups such as the Nation of Islam vowed that they would continue patrols with or without police assistance.

The second broad approach to fighting drugs involves *treatment and prevention* (Weingart, 1993). Traditional drug treatment programs are scarce in poor neighborhoods. Many are prohibitively expensive for indigent users, unless a judge mandates government-paid treatment as a condition of a probation sentence (12-step programs such as Narcotics Anonymous are notable exceptions). Most antidrug programs in this category emphasize prevention. The St. Louis Youth Prevention Education Program intervened with adolescents in the early stages of drug use, before their behavior had led to arrest and conviction (National Center for Neighborhood Enterprise, 1990). Program staff referred clients and their parents to an afterschool counseling program held every weekday for 10 weeks. The program founders designed the intervention to provide participants with information on drug abuse, to help them develop tools for coping with stress, and to build their self-esteem.

Some education programs are intended to inoculate kids against drugs at an early age. The Los Angeles No Dope Transformation Project was a response to a California attorney general's report that indicated that 10% of sixth graders were using drugs and alcohol on a regular basis. The program, later integrated into the curriculum of the Compton School District, uses puppet shows and movies to warn children as young as 5 years old of the dangers of drugs (National Center for Neighborhood Enterprise, 1990).

Other community efforts provide at-risk youth with alternatives to drugs. Many of these initiatives open up school facilities after hours or encourage wholesome recreational opportunities for neighborhood youth. One of the most innovative was the southeast Washington, D.C., Peter Bug Shoe Repair Academy, located in a reclaimed drug-shooting gallery. Peter Bug, who is a master cobbler, took in dozens of students from the streets each year and trained them to repair shoes. In the process, he exposed youth to an extended family of role models who acted as teachers, friends, and parents (National Center for Neighborhood Enterprise, 1990).

A third approach to fighting drugs involves *community building* (Weingart, 1993). Many antidrug groups have attempted to improve the quality of the physical environment by razing abandoned buildings, getting rid of trash, removing graffiti, and repainting neighborhood structures. Through neighborhood renovation, antidrug activists communicate the message that the neighborhood is a place for the respectable activities of local residents and not a hospitable environment for drug dealers or other criminals (Skogan, 1990).

An innovative variation on the community-building approach was taken by Reach Everyone Administer Care and Hope (REACH), sponsored by Detroit's Twelfth Street Missionary Baptist Church. The congregation bought crack houses, which were mostly abandoned or owned by the city. After removing the drug sellers and users, they rehabilitated the houses, using community residents with construction skills as supervisors and unemployed workers as construction laborers. They then sold the renovated homes to local families, whose down payment was the "sweat equity" they earned in the rehab process (Kates, 1990).

The most radical example of the community-building approach comes from South Philadelphia. Community organizers there used an existing network of block captains to go door-to-door to conduct referendums on what values residents wanted to uphold on their block. The community organizers believed that this process was necessary because residents of low-income, high-crime neighborhoods have more diverse values than middle-class suburbanites and are less likely to agree about what constitutes permissible behavior. The organizers found, for example, that many residents of low-income neighborhoods had little patience for noise and rowdy behavior associated with youth clustering in the streets, but others were more tolerant of such behavior, emphasizing the lack of recreational facilities for youth and the need for them to have a place to congregate. After a mandate for neighborhood values was reached, the organizers worked with block residents to translate that mandate into action (Davis, Smith, Lurigio, & Skogan, 1991).

Origins of Community Antidrug Initiatives

Community antidrug efforts usually begin in response to the overt sales of drugs on the streets, which is typically accompanied by rowdy behavior, a flow of outsiders into the neighborhood, threats to residents, home break-ins, and robberies. Often a single critical episode incites community residents to take action against drugs. In Chicago, church members started the Near Northwest Neighborhood Network following an incident in which a parishioner was caught in the cross fire between rival gang members. In San Diego, housewives and mothers organized the City Heights Residents' Anticrime Committee in response to 22 shootings within a block-and-one-half area in less than 2 months. Organizers said that they were "fed up with the neighborhood feeling like a war zone" (quote from unpublished data from Davis, Smith, Lurigio, & Skogan, 1991).

Not all communities that suffer the damaging effects of the drug trade organize antidrug initiatives; in many drug-ridden neighborhoods residents never make a serious, concerted response to drugs.

As we discussed earlier in the chapter, community crime prevention experts have found that higher income levels characterize communities that are likely to produce an anticrime response. Rosenbaum (1987) noted in a review of neighborhood watch programs,

> There is a long line of scholarly work on urban neighborhoods that suggests that informal social control is less likely to develop in low income and culturally heterogeneous neighborhoods. . . . Neighborhoods that need the most help (i.e., have the most crime problems) will be the least receptive to such programs because these residential areas are characterized by suspicion, distrust, hostility, and a lack of shared norms regarding appropriate public behavior. (pp. 114-115)

In sharp contrast to the academic literature on community anticrime efforts, media accounts often highlight local antidrug programs that arise in low-income, high-crime neighborhoods. Similarly, in their case studies, Weingart et al. (1994) report that "innovative strategies flourished in desolate and disorganized neighborhoods—neighborhoods characterized by poverty and disadvantage, with seemingly few resources to draw upon" (p. 2).

Why is there inconsistency between traditional community anticrime wisdom and more recent anecdotal accounts of community antidrug efforts? In covering community antidrug programs in low-income neighborhoods, were the media focusing on exceptions rather than the rule? Or were conclusions about the community anticrime programs of the 1970s limited to only those programs and inapplicable to the community antidrug efforts of the 1980s?

Davis, Smith, Lurigio, and Skogan (1991) sought some answers to these questions. They collected data in 36 neighborhoods in six cities, Chicago, San Francisco, Philadelphia, Atlanta, Houston, and Newark, that were the subject of studies involving large-sample surveys conducted between 1978 and 1983. The surveys shared a common core of questions about neighborhood demographics, victimization, and residents' perceptions of neighborhood problems. The neighborhoods represented a broad spectrum of the urban United States: They were 54% African American or Hispanic, 19% elderly, 51% renters, and 8% unemployed.

In the 36 neighborhoods, the investigators also collected data on drug problems by questioning positionally defined informants (i.e., city council members, police district commanders and neighborhood relations officers, and leaders of community organizations) about current events and conditions. For each neighborhood, investigators averaged residents' responses to construct area-level indicators of drug problems and community responses to those problems. They then merged current neighborhood profiles with information from the earlier resident surveys.

Davis, Smith, Lurigio, and Skogan (1991) isolated factors that predicted "confrontational activism" in all of the neighborhoods. Confrontational activism included citizen patrols, antidrug marches or rallies, evictions of drug dealers or users, and demolition or restoration of drug buildings. In an analysis of several variables, the researchers found three factors that predicted neighborhood mobilization against drugs. Not surprisingly, community antidrug activism was related to neighborhood drug problems (see Table 3.1). Neighborhoods with more serious drug and crime problems were more active than those with less serious drug problems.

What was surprising, however, was that confrontational activism was more likely in less-affluent, higher-crime, black or Hispanic neighborhoods. Even after taking into account the fact that poorer neighborhoods are likely to have more severe drug problems, activism was more vibrant in poorer neighborhoods. This finding directly contradicts the long-standing belief in the community crime prevention field that anticrime programs are not likely to appear in poor areas (e.g., Greenberg et al., 1982; Rosenbaum, 1986). Furthermore, it contradicts the results of Skogan (1989), who found that when all other factors are controlled, more affluent areas are better organized than poor ones. Davis, Smith, Lurigio, and Skogan's (1991) finding was all the more striking because community activism was more apparent in poor neighborhoods even after taking into account the fact that poor neighborhoods are more likely to have severe drug problems.

Davis, Smith, Lurigio, and Skogan also found that antidrug activism was strongly related to a neighborhood's capacity to instigate marches, rallies, and citizen patrols. Block clubs were crucial:

TABLE 3.1 Regression Analysis of Indices of Confrontational Activism

Variable	Beta	Sig.
Drug problems index	.27	.08
Block organization	.35	.01
Area affluence	−.33	.04

NOTE: There were 36 cases for each measure, adjusted $R^2 = .45$.

There was a substantial correlation between estimates of the percentage of area blocks that were covered by block associations and later reports of antidrug activities. Another important element was the existence of a local church, neighborhood improvement, or umbrella antidrug organization. In Baltimore, for example, a strong antidrug effort arose in the Butchers Hill neighborhood, which grew out of the Butchers Hill Association, a community organization established in the 1970s to improve neighborhood appearance and quality of life. Similarly, in Detroit, the antidrug effort REACH evolved from the established community and social agenda of the Twelfth Street Missionary Baptist Church (Kates, 1990).

Taken together, the three factors in the Davis, Smith, Lurigio, and Skogan (1991) study—drug pervasiveness, income, and organizational capacity—explained nearly half of the differences in the community activism measure. The conclusion that low-income, high-crime neighborhoods are more likely than middle-class neighborhoods to spawn community antidrug initiatives was noted as well in the Kennedy School case studies of community antidrug programs: Weingart et al. (1994) concluded that, "Useful forms of citizen antidrug efforts have emerged in a variety of neighborhoods, including those seriously affected by crime and violence that were previously not considered likely to engage in this form of community action" (p. 1).

What other factors determine why community initiatives start in some neighborhoods rather than in others? One explanation is that some communities receive a boost from antidrug interest groups. In other words, many community antidrug efforts are not strictly indigenous. The primary interest group is often the local police. For example, Philadelphia's Let's Clean It Up (LCIU), which we describe in detail at the end of the chapter, was created as part of a police inspector's master plan. He targeted one neighborhood in each police district where a serious drug problem persisted and where he believed great potential existed for neighbors to organize. In the targeted areas, the police disrupted drug dealers through buy-and-bust operations (see Chapter 5) and drug house eradications (see Chapter 6). In the 17th District, the police inspector worked with community organizers to channel community outrage over drug dealers' shooting of a 4-year-old boy. The police, church leaders, and professional organizers sponsored community meetings, held vigils, and boarded up vacant buildings that addicts and dealers had used as drug hangouts. A local woman who was visibly involved in antidrug activities was offered support if she would take on a leadership role in this new venture. She agreed, and Let's Clean It Up was born.

In Miami, Operation Push Out the Pushers (POP) was completely a top-down creation of the local Urban League. Miami's Liberty City section was notorious for rampant drug and crime problems. The head of Miami's Urban League wanted to do something to curb drug trafficking but was discouraged by a long history of distrust between the police and the community and the extreme violence of the drug dealers. The Urban League formed a task force composed of representatives of key city agencies—police, fire, sanitation, and zoning. The task force coordinated police activity, cited run-down properties for code violations, demolished abandoned properties, and cleaned trash from empty lots. Attempts to solicit help from church and community groups met with only mixed success: The local population was highly transient and the few existing community organizations were poorly staffed and largely inactive. Nonetheless, Operation POP made significant progress in curbing visible drug activity in Liberty City.

Weingart et al. (1992) suggest that a top-down approach to antidrug efforts does not take hold in a community as effectively as does a grassroots effort. Extensive media coverage characterized Philadelphia's United Neighbors Against Drugs as remarkably successful against drug dealers. But the program was established largely through the efforts of professional community organizers (all but one of the founders lived outside the Norris Square neighborhood where the program was active), and it withered away after they turned to other interests (Simon, 1991). Weingart et al. (1992) describe the similar history of the Brotherhood Crusade Program in Los Angeles. Many grassroots efforts also eventually cease activities after initial successes against drug dealers. (We return to the issue of program longevity later in this chapter.)

Although the genesis of some antidrug initiatives can be attributed to the work of community organizers, the vast majority are begun by individual area residents, who are often politically connected and experienced organizers. They know how to get neighbors motivated and how to overcome the inertia in city bureaucracies, but they are still "of the community." They are local people who simply get to the point where they say, "Not here you don't" to drug dealers. In many cases, these dedicated individuals are critical to the development and maintenance of community antidrug efforts.

Seattle's Operation Results Program provides an excellent illustration of the crucial role that a motivated individual can play in an antidrug effort. Raw anger at seeing his neighborhood taken over by drugs led a local candle maker to confront drug dealers. He undermined their business by standing near them and taking pictures as they tried to sell dope. Although he was expelled from his local community anticrime organization and criticized by the media for his confrontational and dangerous methods, he persevered and made a real difference in his neighborhood (Davis, Smith, Lurigio, & Skogan, 1991).

Factors such as neighborhood socioeconomic status, drug problems, and organizational capacity may help to prepare a neighborhood for organized antidrug efforts. But without at least one determined individual who is willing to invest substantial time and energy and who can weather initial disappointments and obstacles, an organization may never form even under the best neighborhood conditions.

Integration of Community Antidrug
Efforts With Larger Efforts to Fight Drugs

Roehl et al. (1995) report that most of the community antidrug initiatives they identified included coordinated efforts with a variety of other organizations and agencies. The vast majority of community groups worked with local law enforcement agencies on a regular basis, and more than half had established relationships with social services agencies, schools, or other community organizations. Most community efforts are well integrated with the antidrug efforts of local police or larger, umbrella antidrug organizations. Other community efforts operate independently, often because their leaders or constituents harbor a deep-seated distrust of the official power structure. Both kinds of programs can make a difference, but programs integrated into the political structure certainly have a wider range of resources at their disposal.

Community initiatives in which citizens work on their own tend to use more confrontational methods. Nation of Islam efforts in Washington, D.C., and Brooklyn began as the isolated actions of a small group of members of local mosques. The police were not consulted about the antidrug efforts in either area. Complaints of mosque members threatening drug dealers led police to intervene on the side of the dealers. After a while, the Nation of Islam members and police called a truce and eventually the Nation of Islam efforts won the respect and support of the police (Davis, 1989).

Seattle's Operation Results is another illustration of a community patrol program in which participants do not work with the police or other neighborhood organizations. Undaunted by initial media and anticrime group criticism of its confrontational style, Operation Results has been instrumental in cleaning up several neighborhoods in the Ranier Valley. The program is so successful, in fact, that former President Bush designated it as one of the "thousand points of light." With success comes respectability, and Operation Results came to share important information with the Seattle police and enjoy favorable relations with other local anticrime groups.

210 Stanton, an antidrug program based in a Section 8 apartment building (privately owned, with government-subsidized rents) on New York City's Lower East Side, is a good example of a community-based initiative integrated with other local antidrug efforts. One of the residents became upset when she observed blatant drug sales and prostitution in the hallways of the building. Professional organizers gave her guidance on community organizing and put her

in contact with a community policing unit within the New York City Police Department. Community police officers cooperated with the tenants of the building to arrest a principal dealer. Tenants then assisted the district attorney's community affairs unit to secure a high bail and stiff sentence for the dealer (Powers, 1993).

Do Community Antidrug
Initiatives Make a Difference?

Measuring the impact of community antidrug efforts turns out to be difficult. The aim of these initiatives is simple: to reduce or eliminate visible drug sales and use in a block, a group of contiguous blocks, or a larger area. The best way, scientifically speaking, to measure the effects of community initiatives is to conduct an experiment or quasi-experiment (Cook & Campbell, 1979) in which an initiative is implanted in one or more neighborhoods and not implanted in other neighborhoods that are otherwise comparable to those receiving the initiatives. Ideally, the neighborhoods would be selected to receive the initiatives through a random assignment process.

The trouble with such an approach is that even if it could be successfully implemented, the results of the research would be applicable only to *implanted* programs, not to truly grassroots efforts arising from the community itself. And this could be a very important distinction in terms of resident participation, program longevity, and many other factors likely to be important to understanding program effects on the drug trade. To study truly indigenous community antidrug efforts, researchers can only begin their work after they discover that citizens in a particular neighborhood have begun to act. At that point, the researchers can try to reconstruct preprogram drug activity and compare it to current drug activity, or they can compare current drug activity in the affected neighborhood with drug activity in another, similar neighborhood. Neither approach is very good, but with *indigenous* community efforts, they are the best we can do.

One way to assess drug activity in an impact evaluation of community initiatives is to use police data on drug arrests and complaints. But police data are inherently limited because they do not include incidents that residents fail to report. The intended effect of an antidrug program, such as Boston's Drop-a-Dime, is to increase residents' watchfulness of street activities and their willingness to report drug activity. Therefore, an increase in complaints and arrests suggests program success even though, typically, increases in these indicators may also mean that drug activity is on the rise. Another limitation of using police data to evaluate community initiatives is that many police departments do not aggregate data on complaints of drug activity, and few departments are able to produce information for particular neighborhoods within their districts (Davis, Smith, & Hillenbrand, 1991).

Given the serious shortcomings of police data, the best way to study the effects of indigenous antidrug efforts is to examine how they affect residents' perceptions of drug activity. Such a study was included in Davis, Smith, Lurigio, and Skogan's (1991) work. In neighborhoods served by four exemplary programs, we conducted telephone surveys to compare residents' perceptions of current neighborhood conditions with their recollections of preprogram conditions and with the perceptions of residents of a comparison neighborhood in the same city. The investigators assumed that a program effect was present if residents' perceptions in the program neighborhood changed for the better over time while residents' perceptions in the comparison neighborhood remained constant or became worse over time.

The telephone survey contained questions in six content domains adapted from previous studies on crime prevention (Lewis & Salem, 1981; Skogan, 1990; Skogan & Maxfield, 1981). The first set of questions asked about *neighborhood decline*. Residents were instructed to rate the severity of signs of social disorder such as drug sales, prostitution, public drunkenness, and noisy bars; signs of physical decay such as trash, vandalism, and abandoned cars; and crime problems such as robbery, assault, and burglary. The second set of questions measured *fear of crime*. Participants were asked how safe they feel in their neighborhood when home alone during the day or when out alone at night. The third set of questions examined *informal social control*. These questions explored the willingness of residents to challenge antisocial behavior of neighborhood youths and to remove visible signs of disorder and decay. The fourth set of questions investigated *social cohesion*, probing shared neighborhood concerns, values, and vigilance. The fifth set of questions measured *neighborhood empowerment* by assessing residents' perceptions of their ability to solve problems and achieve positive changes in their neighborhood. The sixth set of questions queried respondents regarding their *satisfaction with the neighborhood* in meeting their needs and providing them with adequate police services. Other items in the questionnaire asked about program awareness and contact.

The four community antidrug initiatives chosen for the impact assessment were selected by the researchers as exemplary from 147 programs nominated by local experts in 20 cities. The programs were also chosen to maximize diversity. Philadelphia's Let's Clean It Up ran a drug hotline and sponsored efforts to make the physical environment more attractive (e.g., by cleaning up trash and graffiti) and safer (e.g., by installing alley gates to prevent access by nonresidents). This program, located in a poor but stable African American neighborhood, was given considerable assistance from the police and local community organizers. In contrast, Baltimore's Butchers Hill Association used a van to patrol a neighborhood undergoing gentrification. When drug activity was spotted, local police were notified. Although the neighborhood was mixed ethnically and economically, the organization's many participants were largely white professionals with good connections in local government and ample political savvy. Seattle's Operation Results also operated a mobile patrol with members who photographed and harassed drug dealers but did not contact the police. The organization consisted of a handful of individuals who worked autonomously, with limited community support. Miami's Operation POP was a top-down effort created by the local Urban League and city officials, with limited cooperation from local residents. The program's methods primarily involved building code enforcement, enhanced police patrols, and neighborhood cleanup.

Comparison neighborhoods were picked because they were similar to the program areas on official crime statistics, resident demographics, socioeconomic status, and housing stock. The survey data generally showed few preexisting differences between program and comparison neighborhoods with regard to resident characteristics or resident perceptions along the six dimensions described earlier.

The researchers analyzed impact data separately for each site, comparing program areas to comparison areas and current perceptions of the neighborhood to perceptions of the neighborhood 2 years prior. The critical test of program impact was whether the program made a difference over the prior 2 years in any of the study's outcome variables.

The results strongly indicated that the programs had a favorable effect on respondents' perceptions of crime, drugs, and disorder. Table 3.2 shows that significant Treatment × Time interactions appeared across the four cities. Moreover, simple effects analyses revealed that the changes were consistently in the expected directions—neighborhood improvement was seen only in the program areas. All of the programs reduced fear of crime; three of the four programs enhanced social control and cohesion; and two of the four programs increased resident empowerment and neighborhood satisfaction and reduced signs of physical decay. Figure 3.1 graphically shows program effects on fear of crime. Fear declined in all four program neighborhoods over time. In contrast, fear remained relatively constant in the comparison neighborhoods.

In general, the results suggest that the wider support that programs enjoy in the community, the greater their success. The greatest number of significant effects were seen in Baltimore, where program recognition and contact was highest. But it is noteworthy that even Seattle's Operation Results had significant effects, even though just 4% of survey respondents had ever heard of this tiny program and none had participated in its activities. This observation is encouraging in light of Roehl et al.'s (1995) finding that participation in community antidrug initiatives is generally low. Greater participation of citizens is certainly desirable and can enhance effectiveness, but there appear to be substantial inroads that programs can make even without widespread community support.

The fact that community antidrug initiatives can have significant effects on neighborhoods even without widespread community participation flies in the face of conventional wisdom. In large measure, this seemingly anomalous finding may stem from differences in the nature of the crimes targeted by modern antidrug

TABLE 3.2 Program Effectiveness: Treatment × Time Interactions

Scale	Seattle	Philadelphia	Baltimore	Miami
Social disorder	<1	2.16	7.43***	<1
Physical decay	<1	1.32	15.63***	2.92*
Crime problems	<1	<1	8.33***	1.13
Fear of crime	4.67**	8.29****	8.29****	5.35**
Social control	1.43	2.94*	9.92****	4.29***
Social cohesion	7.49****	3.14*	3.09*	<1
Empowerment	2.14	4.58**	11.07****	<1
Satisfaction	4.40**	6.18***	1.81	<1

NOTE: Figures are F values.
$*p < .1; **p < .05; ***p < .01; ****p < .005.$

programs versus those targeted by earlier anticrime programs. Drug selling is a different sort of criminal act than the muggings and burglaries that were targeted in the 1970s and early 1980s by community anticrime groups. In burglaries and muggings, criminals—often with unknown identities—pick targets seemingly at random from a neighborhood. To have an effect on these crimes, community anticrime programs had to be able to elicit behavioral changes in large portions of the community: Lots of people had to surveil and be willing to report crimes if relatively infrequent and unpredictable events like burglary and robbery were to be affected; only seldom was such participation achieved. Rosenbaum (1987) notes that, "the typical levels of participation in watch programs are hardly sufficient to produce occasional surveillance" (p. 125).

In sharp contrast, street drug sales are conducted from a relatively stationary location (a street corner, store, or dwelling) and sellers are not difficult to spot. Particular sellers may change location from time to time, as dictated by police and community pressure, but sellers must be easy to locate by both established customers and passers-by looking for drugs. Drug sellers, in other words, must be semipublic and semivisible figures. Because drug sellers engaged in their trade are not difficult to locate, they can be readily targeted by community members interested in curtailing their activity. Sellers

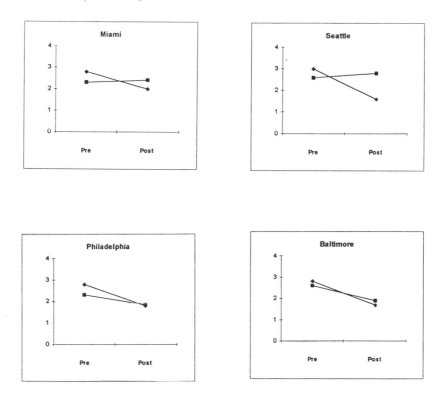

Figure 3.1. Trends in Fear of Crime by City

NOTE: Diamonds represent neighborhoods with antidrug initiatives; squares represent neighborhoods without.

and clients can be harassed in a variety of ways: Police can be called, transactions can be photographed, license plates can be written down, and so forth. These actions can be undertaken *by small groups of concerned citizens.* Large segments of the community do not necessarily have to cooperate.

The study by Davis, Smith, Lurigio, and Skogan (1991) represents the first empirical test of indigenous citizen antidrug initiatives. The results presented in Table 3.2 indicate that such efforts can favorably alter residents' fear of crime, satisfaction with neighborhood, and perceptions of social control, cohesion, and physical disorder. These conclusions must be tempered by two considerations.

First, the programs studied were among the very best in the country. The best way to interpret the study results is that community antidrug initiatives *can* make a difference—not that any particular program is likely to make a difference. Second, it should be emphasized that neighborhood-based efforts typically do not attempt to reduce drug activity at the macro level. Rather, residents are simply trying to get it out of their neighborhood. It is highly likely that drug sales are merely displaced by such efforts, not eliminated.

Researchers at Harvard's Kennedy School reached similar conclusions in its case studies of community antidrug initiatives. The Kennedy School researchers did not collect their own data but, based on police data and other publicly available data, concluded that community antidrug efforts "can be an effective and viable entity in combating drug problems" (Weingart et al., 1994, p. 1).

Issues for Future Research

Important policy questions remain to be answered about community antidrug programs. Although we know that programs have originated in unlikely places, we also know that residents in many affected neighborhoods have not organized against drugs. We need to know more about the social-psychological factors that encourage program development and maintenance. Community psychologists have started research in this direction by examining the effects of contextual factors, such as sense of community, on perceptions of block problems and on neighborhood organization (Chavis & Wandersman, 1990; Perkins, Florin, Rich, Wandersman, & Chavis, 1990). But researchers are finding as well that neighborhoods with successful organizations often have a strong "take-charge" individual who has the commitment and interpersonal skills to motivate his or her neighbors. Ultimately, we may be able to answer the question, "Do organizations form in a particular neighborhood because of the hard work and persistence of dedicated individuals, or do they form because certain conditions make the neighborhood ripe for organizing?"

Although we know from media accounts and studies that many programs have emerged in response to the drug crisis of the late

1980s, we do not know how many have lasted. Even though antidrug organizations are more likely to form in poor neighborhoods, are such programs as hardy as programs in mixed-income or middle-class neighborhoods? When programs do become inactive, is it because they solved their target problems, as some of the case studies of Weingart et al. (1992) suggest? If programs die out for other reasons, it would be useful to understand the reasons and to learn whether any actions can be taken to increase program longevity. It may turn out that programs persist, in part, because they expand their agenda beyond crime, as Skogan (1988) and others suggest. In that case, the government should encourage new antidrug programs to adopt multiple agendas and give them technical assistance in doing so.

Finally, anecdotal data from citizens who participate in community antidrug efforts suggests that these actions often displace drug activity to other neighborhoods. More systematic investigation is required to determine whether activists only fob off the problem on their less-organized neighbors or whether they also cause temporary disruptions in local drug trafficking or more permanent disruptions in the activities of marginal street dealers.

Researchers have substantiated what the media have been reporting for several years: Residents in low-income communities across the country have made drugs their focal concern and they are making a difference. This should be heartening news to a federal government still intent on waging a war on drugs. More research needs to be done on ways in which the government can support the antidrug efforts of private citizens.

Profile of a Successful Program: Philadelphia's Let's Clean It Up

Let's Clean It Up (LCIU) is a successful, yet seemingly simple, neighborhood antidrug effort. Its primary activities include coordinating reports of drug activity from a network of older residents and getting people of all ages involved in cleaning up and maintaining their neighborhood. The program's initiation and continued success are the results of a cooperative endeavor, drawing on the energy and determination of a strong leader, the resources of the local police district, and the knowledge and expertise of community organizers associated with an umbrella antidrug organization.

Philadelphia's 17th District is known as a "bad" district among the police. Drugs and crime are commonplace. Shootings connected to the drug trade are a regular occurrence. Even the police captain in charge of the area has admitted, "You're liable to get robbed, beaten, or stabbed in the 17th District" (quoted in Davis, Smith, Lurigio, & Skogan, 1991, p. 19).

Longtime area residents can still remember when things were different—when the district was a quiet area of working-class home owners who kept their front steps scrubbed and oversaw one another's children. Things have changed a lot. Many of the row houses are not being kept up the way they were years ago. Somewhere along the line, the sense of community disappeared. "This isn't the kind of neighborhood where people stop at each other's house for coffee," lamented one longtime resident (quoted in Davis, Smith, Lurigio, & Skogan, 1991, p. 19). Even today, however, most of the homes are owner occupied. A lot of senior citizens who have deep roots in the neighborhood still live in the 17th District. Although the area remains overwhelmingly African American, Asians have recently begun to settle there.

The small area (just eight square blocks centering around 17th & Tasker Streets) where LCIU operates is fairly typical of the 17th District. It is not the worst part of the district: Abandonment of residential units—several per block in some sections—has not occurred with great frequency around 17th and Tasker. But drugs and adolescents hanging out and acting rowdy were a significant problem. LCIU's leader reported that dealers were "at it twenty-four hours a day" in front of her house (quoted in Davis, Smith, Lurigio, & Skogan, 1991, p. 20). People were afraid for their children and could not sleep at night. Buyers drove in from all over the city. The police district captain rated the area around 17th and Tasker among the district's five worst with respect to drugs. The focal point of drug sales was the corner of Colorado and Dickenson streets. Several neighborhood bars also gained local notoriety as centers for drug sales among neighborhood youths, who congregated inside and out.

How LCIU Began. LCIU's story began in July 1988 with the shooting of a 4-year-old boy, hit in the back and paralyzed by a stray bullet fired by a drug dealer. The shooting outraged the community, and a local Baptist minister channeled that outrage to galvanize the community to take action. Through a series of meetings held over the following winter, the Direct Truth Antidrug Coalition was launched.

In the spring, the group was ready to push forward. Accompanied by police, the Baptist minister began the first antidrug march in South Philadelphia from the 17th District station house. At first, residents were hesitant even to participate in the march for fear of retaliation from drug dealers. Cautiously, people watched from behind closed doors, but as the crowd of marchers grew and no violence ensued, more and more people came out to join the rally. By the time the procession ended at the corner of Colorado and Dickenson at 1:30 a.m., more than 100 people had joined the march. The minister led prayers in front of several notorious drug houses and encouraged residents to sit outside or stand on corners to discourage dealing. Drug dealers were shocked.

Soon after the march, the local police captain and community organizers affiliated with Direct Truth held a community meeting at Saint Thomas Aquinas Church. The police offered protection for vigils and the assistance of a community relations officer to help neighborhood residents organize small, localized efforts to fight drugs.

From that point on, Direct Truth and the police worked together to board up vacant houses used by drug dealers and to organize buy-and-bust operations. They also tried to remove other symbols of disorder such as abandoned cars and trash.

Direct Truth organizers approached an elderly woman who had been regularly attending meetings and antidrug rallies. They offered to help her organize her neighborhood if she would take on a leadership role with her neighbors. The woman did not need to be strongly persuaded—"At some point, you just stop being afraid; I decided I'd rather be dead than put up with drug dealers" (quoted in Davis, Smith, Lurigio, & Skogan, 1991, p. 22). LCIU was created in the spring of 1990.

What LCIU Does. LCIU is a small group of determined residents who have been able to accomplish significant changes in their neighborhood because of the group's partnership with Direct Truth and the Philadelphia Police Department's South Division. LCIU's monthly meetings are attended by as few as 10 and as many as 40 people. Nearly all are women; most are middle aged or elderly. About a half dozen of these people constitute the program's core group of supporters.

At weekly meetings, the group's leader brings members up-to-date on recent goings on, and occasionally she invites outside speakers from the city police department, the district attorney's office, the housing department, or other municipal agencies. Members discuss current problems and strategies. At one meeting, plans were discussed to fence in a vacant lot, to discourage graffiti, and to work with a local community organizer to demolish abandoned houses boarded up several months earlier.

At the end of the meetings, members present written complaints (e.g., observations of drug trafficking in the neighborhood). The police train LCIU members on what to include in their reports, and the complaints are often quite detailed, containing names or descriptions of those involved, locations, times of day, and methods of operating. These and other complaints left on LCIU's telephone answering machine are regularly passed along to the police community relations officer, who gives LCIU feedback on what actions are taken in response to the complaints. Members, of course, are also free to call the police directly and do so in urgent situations.

Organizing the neighbors into a telephone tree for reporting drug activity has been LCIU's primary antidrug activity. LCIU also moved against problem properties in the neighborhood. Landowners with drug-dealing tenants were approached and asked to evict them or face court action. LCIU worked with the police and the city Bureau of Licenses and Inspections to evict squatters and seal up abandoned buildings that had become havens for drug activity and prostitution. A series of row houses torched by drug dealers on Bouvier Street was razed. LCIU asked owners of rowdy bars to curb their patrons' behavior. When that did not work, LCIU successfully petitioned the Bureau of Licenses and Inspections to issue citations to the owners.

A collection was taken up among area residents for the installation of iron gates in alleys. These gates were intended to deny drug dealers and other criminals access to their favored routes of escape when confronted by police. One resident tells a story that after the gates were installed, her purse was snatched outside her house. Because the thieves were blocked from escaping through the alley, a group of neighbors was able to catch them and retrieve the purse.

But LCIU's objectives extend well beyond driving out drug dealers. The group is attempting to rebuild the community or at least markedly improve its appearance. If progress can be made toward that goal, participants believe that dealers will not be tempted to set up shop in the future.

During its first summer of operation, LCIU went after trash and graffiti in the neighborhood. Each Saturday, the city sanitation department donated a truck, and residents of the 17th and Tasker area turned out to clean up the streets and seven trash-filled vacant lots. Children got into the act too: Using funds solicited from adult residents, LCIU recruited local youths to sweep the streets, clean graffiti, and paint the outsides of the abandoned buildings that had been sealed up by the city.

Thanks to these LCIU efforts and to the coordinated activities of the police and Direct Truth, local residents believe that drug activity has been greatly diminished. LCIU's leader says that she and the other people on her block are now able to sleep at night uninterrupted by noise from dealers on the street. The local police captain says that the 17th and Tasker area, which was one of the worst five neighborhoods in the district for drug sales, no longer holds that dubious distinction. The bars that were centers of rowdy behavior and drug dealing have calmed down since the citations were issued. Everyone agrees that the neighborhood looks cleaner as a result of LCIU's efforts. In fact, the group was featured in a pictorial section of the newspaper for its use of flower boxes and gardens.

A Three-Legged Stool. LCIU draws strength from its close working relationship with other organizations. LCIU is anything but a simple grassroots antidrug program. It is a product of a deliberate community organizing effort by the police department's South Division and Direct Truth.

The police administrator in charge of the southern half of Philadelphia is a strong proponent of community policing. In the several years he has headed the South Division, he has worked hard to turn around residents' historical antipathy toward the police. These efforts seem to be working: At an awards dinner community residents repeatedly voiced their respect for police administrators.

The South Division commander envisions a partnership between the police and the residents of South Philadelphia, represented in a patchwork of neighborhood anticrime groups covering the entire area. He developed a plan to take back the streets of South Philadelphia. In each police district, he has targeted one neighborhood where a serious drug problem exists and where the residents are organized or show promise of organizing. During Phase 1 of the plan, the police devote the resources necessary to shut down the drug trade through buy-and-bust operations, closing down drug houses and harassing dealers. During Phase 2 of the plan, the district police captains encourage and support emergent community leaders in their efforts to organize neighbors. This support is critical to maintaining and expanding the gains made in Phase 1.

The master plan is coordinated by the South Philadelphia Partnership Service Support Group, a body composed of representatives of the district attorney's office, city and state probation agencies, the Bureau of Licenses and Inspections, the sanitation department, the Philadelphia Antidrug Anti-Violence Network, and other interested agencies. The 17th District is the second district in which the master plan has been implemented to date.

A local community organizer involved in the early development of Direct Truth and the Partnership Service Support Group characterized the community-organizing activities in South Philadelphia as more than just promoting antidrug efforts. He saw it as a process of community building: "You need to fill the vacuum created by removing drug dealers. You need to get people thinking positively about life. It's not enough just to eliminate the negative" (quoted in Davis, Smith, Lurigio, & Skogan, 1991, pp. 26-27).

The strategy adopted in South Philadelphia stands in sharp contrast to antidrug efforts in North Philadelphia. There, Herman Wrice and his original organization, Mantua Against Drugs, gained national attention and admiration (including a visit from former

President Bush) by adopting a high-profile approach that involved confronting dealers on the streets and battering down the doors of abandoned buildings used as sites for drug sales. This type of approach requires only a small nucleus of committed supporters and typically generates shallow community support.

The organizers in South Philadelphia worked to establish neighborhood organizations with broad resident support to work on a range of issues affecting the community, not solely the drug problem. Their philosophy is consistent with the accepted belief of community organizers everywhere that groups cannot survive and grow if they focus exclusively on reducing crime.

South Philadelphia organizers attempted to use a strategy of block-by-block consensus building. "The real law doesn't exist at the neighborhood level. What's 'legal' is whatever neighbors will tolerate," said one organizer. "You need to go door to door to get a mandate for neighborhood values, and build that mandate into action" (quoted in Davis, Smith, Lurigio, & Skogan, 1991, p. 27). A plan was developed to use an existing network of block captains to go door-to-door and, in effect, conduct a referendum on what values residents wanted to uphold. Those values turned out to be somewhat different from one block to the next, because, organizers believed, people in low-income, high-crime neighborhoods have diverse values and are less likely to agree on what constitutes acceptable behavior on their streets than are middle-class suburbanites. After they reached a consensus on values, the organizers asked all the residents to enforce them.

The community organizers at Direct Truth supply LCIU with community-organizing skills and with contacts and know-how in dealing with agencies such as sanitation, licensing and inspection, and the water and electric companies. Direct Truth also has supported LCIU in many other ways, from helping to organize rallies and vigils, to coordinating efforts to seal up or raze abandoned houses, to operating a food bank and counseling program for addicts. The police have also intervened with city agencies on behalf of LCIU. In addition, they have removed abandoned autos left on the street, evicted squatters from vacant buildings, conducted buy-and-bust operations, and provided protection for participants in marches and vigils.

LCIU receives a big boost from the South Philadelphia Partnership Service Support Group. Through this support group, leaders of neighborhood organizations are brought together once a month to exchange stories about problems, methods, and successes. The group acts to promote rapid cross-fertilization of ideas. Furthermore, it gives neighborhood leaders a sense that they are not alone and provides them with accolades for their triumphs.

Plans for the Future. Once the neighborhood drug problem was under control, LCIU's interest shifted to helping rebuild the community, which demanded greater involvement in the local political arena. One example of that shift is the organization's current attempt to become an advocate for neighborhood interests in a private developer's plan to build 43 units of low-income housing on several adjacent vacant lots owned by the city. Residents are resisting the plan for the complex in its present form. They are concerned about high-density population and the amount of traffic (both pedestrian and auto) that such a complex would draw to the neighborhood.

Those in attendance at one LCIU meeting were initially divided on whether to lobby their city council member for a scaled-down version of the housing proposal or for the construction of a community center. In the end, the group decided to explore a third option that certainly no one would have predicted at the meeting's outset: They decided to set up an appointment with their council member to discuss a scaled-down version of the low-income housing plan with LCIU acting as the developer. A neighborhood resident knowledgeable in developing low-income housing argued that the profits from the rental units could be used to rehabilitate abandoned houses in the neighborhood.

Other items on LCIU's agenda include obtaining city approval to construct a "tot lot" on the site of the row homes that recently burned and were razed and to install better street lighting in the area. To take on these projects, LCIU is prepared to pursue the same kinds of fund-raising efforts—block parties, bake sales, and neighborhood outings—as it did to finance the installation of alley gates.

Finally, LCIU is planning to expand its base of support in the community. The organization's leaders admit that it has not been easy to motivate people to improve their neighborhood. They have had to fight against fear (members have been the target of numerous threats) and apathy of area residents, some of whom are involved with drugs or have family members involved with drugs. To date, LCIU has relied on monthly fliers and limited door-to-door and telephone canvassing to generate support. Now, most area residents know and support LCIU. Nonetheless, even at recent meetings, younger residents and men have been conspicuously absent.

4. Implanted Community Antidrug Programs

In the previous chapter, we discussed indigenous community antidrug initiatives. This chapter is devoted to programs that are implanted in communities, usually through government intervention. Many implanted programs are created when communities respond to requests for proposals for antidrug initiatives. Other times, established community organizations receive funds from a national program to expand and strengthen existing antidrug activities. Implanted programs are far better funded than indigenous community antidrug initiatives. They are usually conducted on a much larger scale, targeting entire cities rather than single neighborhoods. Typically, implanted programs involve extensive coordination among multiple local organizations and are dominated by public or politically powerful social service agencies—not grassroots community organizations.

Implanted programs can be an evaluator's dream. With indigenous programs, a researcher studying the impact of a program cannot take measurements to examine the conditions in the neighborhood before program implementation. Some information, for example, police data on drug arrests and complaints prior to program inception, can be obtained, but many important types of preprogram data, including residents' perceptions and observations of social and physical disorder, cannot be collected. In contrast, researchers studying implanted programs know when and where programs will begin and they can implement elaborate pretest-posttest designs to study whether the programs are effective.

From a strictly methodological perspective, researchers can learn much more about program impact by studying implanted programs. However, analyses of implanted programs do not produce valid conclusions about indigenous programs. As Rosenbaum (1988) points out, implanted programs often fail to generate the enthusiastic support from community residents that is achieved with the best indigenous programs. When researchers study implanted programs and find that they have little impact, they can never be sure whether the program model was deficient or whether the program failed because it did not attract sufficient citizen support.

Perhaps because they have been subjected to rigorous evaluation, implanted programs have acquired a bad reputation in the community crime prevention field. Skogan (1990) discusses two experiments in which community organizers tried to implant anticrime programs. In the first, the Ford Foundation funded 10 community organizations in Chicago to launch block watch and other anticrime initiatives. Paid, experienced organizers conducted door-to-door canvassing, sponsored community meetings and workshops, and held leadership training sessions. In spite of these extensive and well-organized efforts, the participation of residents was quite low. Furthermore, no consistent program effects were found on measures of social interaction, neighborhood solidarity, or citizens' efforts to solve neighborhood problems. Even worse, perceptions of social and physical disorder and fear of crime actually increased significantly in targeted neighborhoods.

In the second experiment, the Police Foundation worked with city organizers to implant an anticrime program in Minneapolis. The program's purpose was to create block clubs that would engage in anticrime activities. Professional organizers trained community leaders to organize the clubs by going door-to-door to persuade residents to attend meetings. Every household in the targeted areas was contacted an average of four times. A low initial response in poor, minority areas led the professional organizers to increase their efforts in those neighborhoods. Nonetheless, by the time the project was over, attendance records showed that "people turned out in substantial numbers only in better-off areas . . . where crime problems were not substantial" (Skogan, 1990, p. 148). As in the Chicago experiment, no evidence was found that the program changed residents' willingness to watch the streets or to report information to the police. And no program impact was found on measures of social disorder, physical disorder, crime problems, or fear of crime.

After examining these and other data, Rosenbaum (1986) concluded that some of the central assumptions of community anticrime programs are flawed. In particular, he argued that citizens' cooperation and participation in implanted programs is often low, especially in low-income neighborhoods where the programs are most needed (and where Rosenbaum believed they were unlikely to start on their own); citizens' participation does not necessarily lead to greater social interaction and surveillance in the neighborhood, which are thought to be prerequisites for reducing crime; and increases in social interaction and surveillance do not necessarily lead to less crime or fear of crime.

The obvious question is, Why should implanted antidrug programs work any better than implanted community crime prevention programs designed to reduce robberies, burglaries, and assaults? The answer lies in the argument we presented in Chapter 3: Drug dealers operate in quite a different fashion from that of the kinds of street criminals targeted by anticrime programs of the 1970s and early 1980s. For community anticrime programs to work, behavioral changes had to be elicited from large portions of the community. Programs had to bring neighbors together to interact with one another to cultivate an interest in their community and surveil the neighborhood. But as Rosenbaum (1987) noted, "The typical levels of participation in [neighborhood] watch programs are hardly sufficient to produce occasional surveillance" (p. 125).

In contrast, as we noted in the previous chapter, community antidrug programs capitalize on the fact that drug sales are an open business activity. Because selling locations must be relatively stable, dealers can be effectively harassed by as few as a handful of local residents intent on disrupting their businesses.

The fact that drug sales are a business activity means that community antidrug programs can also work by reducing demand for the product. Programs to educate children or adults about the dangers of illegal drugs pursue a demand reduction approach. Fewer customers translate to lower prices and less profit for drug dealers. In addition, fewer customers mean that fewer people can make a living at selling drugs.

Neither of these strategies—changing the business environment and reducing demand—are applicable to criminals who commit robberies, burglaries, and assaults; both seem to be quite effective against drug dealers. For this reason, it is possible that implanted citizen anticrime programs may meet with more success against drugs than similar programs did against street crimes.

In the remainder of this chapter, we examine four types of implanted community antidrug programs. They are the U.S. Bureau of Justice Assistance Community Responses to Drug Abuse (CRDA), the Center for Substance Abuse Prevention (CSAP) Community Partnership Demonstration Program, the Robert Wood Johnson Foundation Fighting Back Program, and the U.S. Bureau of Justice Assistance Weed and Seed Initiative. The chapter concludes with a case study.

Community Responses
to Drug Abuse (CRDA)

In 1988, when CRDA was created, the National Crime Prevention Council and the National Training and Information Center requested funding from the U.S. Bureau of Justice Assistance for antidrug activities (Rosenbaum, Bennett, Lindsay, & Wilkinson, 1994). The funding was targeted for 10 community-based organizations across the country that addressed multiple local problems and had experienced some success in building communities and developing leaders. This is an important point: Because significant antidrug organizing had gone on prior to federal funding, these sites had a better chance of succeeding than they would have if they had started from scratch when the federal dollars became available. Nearly all of the organizations were situated in poor neighborhoods with serious gang violence, drug sales, and other criminal activity.

A technical assistance team from the National Crime Prevention Council and the National Training and Information Center strongly encouraged the 10 participating organizations to engage in a formal, community-based planning process. The team hosted a conference that focused on program planning and development. They recommended that the participating organizations form a multiagency task force to assist in the development of work plans. Most of the organizations relied on members and staff to develop the plans rather than on professionals from outside the organization.

Over a 6-month period, members of the technical assistance team reviewed drafts of the plans and assisted each of the organizations in developing a final strategy. Cluster meetings were held to exchange ideas among programs. The work plans included a specification of community problems as well as goals to address those problems. To develop plans, many organizations conducted needs assessments in their communities and reviewed laws pertaining to nuisance abatement and drug-free zones.

The programs' initial antidrug strategies emphasized law enforcement approaches. Citizens were encouraged to report drug activity, either to the police or to program staff, and their reports were used to identify drug hot spots. Commitments were sought from the police to increase patrol strength. Drug houses were closed by enforcing nuisance abatement laws or building codes. Neighborhood watch and citizen patrol programs were initiated or strengthened. Citizens were encouraged to attend court hearings of local drug dealers to pressure judges into imposing stiff sentences. Lobbying efforts were undertaken to push for the enactment of new laws or to revise old laws on nuisance abatement, asset forfeiture, sale of drug paraphernalia, and drug-free zones.

Most of these law enforcement activities required close cooperation between citizens and the police. Local police administrators played an integral role in the programs by serving on task forces, providing technical assistance, and advocating on the programs' behalf with other groups and agencies. For several organizations, working in cooperation with the police represented a significant departure from their earlier animosity toward law enforcement.

Rosenbaum et al. (1994) indicated that after the first year, a growing recognition of the complexity of the drug problem led program participants away from law enforcement activities toward prevention efforts. Recreational opportunities for neighborhood youth were expanded, parents were educated about drugs, local drug-treatment services were enhanced, and efforts were made in one community to provide a job-training program.

Community Partnership
Demonstration Program

The Center for Substance Abuse Prevention (CSAP) implanted antidrug programs that differed in a number of significant respects from the Community Responses to Drug Abuse (CRDA) programs. First, the scope was much larger: CSAP partnerships were formed in 252 communities across the country. Each site represented an entire community, rather than the discrete neighborhoods targeted by the CRDA program.

Second, the CRDA sites involved action by one organization whereas the CSAP partnerships were comprehensive and coordinated approaches to drug abuse. The partnerships were based on the premise that drug abuse prevention efforts are most successful when they stem from a coalition of organizations in the community. According to Cook and Roehl (1993), the most effective coalitions included representatives from health, social services, welfare, and criminal justice agencies; public schools; government officials; churches; and grassroots community organizations. Furthermore, CSAP funds were not intended to support direct services but rather to "identify service needs in the community, establish community-wide priorities and systems changes, and promote and coordinate drug abuse prevention programs" (Cook & Roehl, 1993, p. 226).

Third, CSAP's goals differed from the goals of CRDA. The CSAP sites were funded to reduce both alcohol and drug abuse. Three of the first 11 sites named alcohol abuse as their primary target. The CSAP partnerships attempted expressly to reduce drug use among youth. They also sought to decrease alcohol and drug abuse not just on the streets but in the workplace as well.

Finally, CSAP's program methods differed from CRDA's. The CSAP program took a public health approach to the problem of drug abuse. The CSAP partnerships emphasized public education, including media coverage of the program, pamphlets, community workshops, public service announcements, and displays at community functions. In addition, the partnerships were active in several youth initiatives ranging from recreational programs to antidrug education sessions to esteem-building activities. Moreover, partnerships became involved in improving linkages among service organizations. According to Cook and Roehl (1993), the kinds of law enforcement activities that were so prominent in the early days of the CRDA programs were almost completely absent from the CSAP programs.

Fighting Back Program

The Robert Wood Johnson Foundation Fighting Back Program was one of the most ambitious implanted community antidrug initiatives ever launched. Each participating municipality planned and implemented a communitywide system of responses to illicit drug and alcohol abuse, which incorporated public awareness; prevention programs; early intervention, assessment, and referral; and treatment and aftercare (Klitzner, 1993).

Communities were selected for Fighting Back awards through a highly competitive process. Fifteen communities were ultimately chosen from more than 300 proposals and given 2 years to develop implementation plans. Thirteen of the 15 were given funds to implement the plans over a 5-year period.

The Fighting Back sites were quite diverse. Although eligibility was limited to communities with populations between 150,000 and 250,000 residents, some sites included small cities, others consisted of sections of larger cities, and still others included several counties. Applicant organizations ranged from executive branches of government to intergovernmental associations, to the United Way, and to individual social services organizations.

Similiar to the other types of implanted programs discussed in this chapter, the Fighting Back programs employed a community-driven approach to curbing illegal drug abuse. In each case, the funder left it up to participating communities to define the specific problems they wanted to address and the specific methods they wanted to employ to solve those problems. Most of the Fighting Back sites successfully garnered additional funding to implement specific components of their overall strategies.

Fighting Back is based on the concept of comprehensive, community-based programming. The program's overall vision includes all aspects of the substance abuse problem, the entire continuum of care, and multiple target populations. The public health approach implemented by Fighting Back programs included education, prevention, and treatment of illegal drug use and alcohol abuse. A number of the sites involved neighborhood centers that brought these services closer to needy residents.

In their vision and scope, Fighting Back programs are much closer in nature to the CSAP partnerships than to the CRDA programs. Both adopted a public health approach to the problem of drug abuse and both are dominated by powerful public and private agencies rather than grassroots community groups.

Weed and Seed Initiative

Weed and Seed is the most recent of the ambitious implanted antidrug programs discussed here. Initiated in 1991 by the U.S. Bureau of Justice Assistance, Weed and Seed is "a means of mobilizing a large and varied array of resources in a comprehensive, coordinated effort to control crime and drugs and improve the quality of life in targeted high crime neighborhoods" (Roehl, 1995, p. 1). Weed and Seed is distinguished by its philosophy, which explicitly states that successful antidrug efforts must involve a strong law enforcement response linked with education, prevention, treatment, and community revitalization efforts. Weed and Seed funds were given in roughly equal amounts to 19 cities, differing dramatically in size from 2.8 million to 35,000. Sites varied in racial composition (some were predominantly African American, some Hispanic, and some non-Hispanic white). Crime rates also differed substantially among the Weed and Seed, although all were reported to have suffered from relatively high rates of substance abuse; drug trafficking, including open-air markets; and drug-related crime and violence (Roehl, 1995).

Weed and Seed programs were definitely top-down approaches to fighting drugs. Most sites targeted street-level dealing of small amounts of drugs and had local steering committees to guide program development and policy. Weed Committees and Seed Committees were responsible for implementing policies and strategies. Participants at many sites developed smaller working groups to direct day-to-day operations. A Weed and Seed coordinator, a Weed coordinator, and a Seed coordinator were responsible for carrying out directives of the committees. The various positions were filled primarily with staff from local law enforcement agencies, city agencies, and social service organizations.

Although Weed and Seed is supposed to encompass both law enforcement and community revitalization efforts, in fact, the former has received far greater emphasis than the latter. Law enforcement activities have received the lion's share of the monies, with nearly 80% going to overtime and equipment for police or prosecution agencies (Roehl, 1995). Law enforcement monies have been spent to promote traditional police antidrug, antigun, and antigang tactics; community policing; and prosecution strategies aimed at removing the worst offenders from neighborhoods.

What Have Implanted
Antidrug Programs Achieved?

Evaluations of the four types of implanted programs were all comprehensive and generously funded. Researchers combined careful analysis of the implementation process with impact studies of how well specific objectives were achieved by each particular activity at each program site. In addition, Fighting Back evaluations included sophisticated analysis of community-level indicators of drug abuse. Because each of the demonstration programs covers a lengthy period, only partial research results have been reported to date.

Community Responses to Drug Abuse (CRDA). Initial results from the CRDA program have been quite encouraging. The evaluators used a pretest-posttest control group design, telephoning random samples of residents in target and comparison areas just prior to program implementation and 12 and 15 months after program implementation. The evaluators analyzed pretest and posttest measures in the three sites they considered to have had "the most intensive and successful program implementation" (Rosenbaum & Lavrakas, 1993, p. 3).

Target area residents reported greater awareness of and greater participation in antidrug efforts by local community organizations than did comparison area residents. Perceptions of the neighborhood also differed: Target area residents reported greater satisfaction with their neighborhoods and less desire to move than did residents in comparison areas. Moreover, residents in target areas reported greater social interaction with their neighbors than did controls. Target area residents, however, were not more likely than control respondents to watch their neighbors' homes, which is an essential element of successful anticrime programs. Finally, residents of target areas reported more favorable evaluations of the police than did comparison area respondents.

The results with respect to crime were less encouraging. Residents in target areas were more likely to call the police than were residents in comparison neighborhoods. But there were no differences between the two groups on perceptions of crime or on fear of crime (fear of personal victimization, fear of property victimization, behavioral restrictions, or use of local stores and parks). The interventions did not appear to encourage residents to accept greater responsibility for drug prevention or enhance their feelings of efficacy with regard to solving local problems.

Rosenbaum and Lavrakas's (1993) conclusions about the CRDA implanted programs were similar to Davis, Smith, Lurigio, and Skogan's (1991) conclusions about indigenous programs: Community antidrug programs *can* make a difference in the lives of neighborhood residents.

CSAP Community Partnership. Researchers from the Institute for Social Analysis performed a process evaluation of the Community Partnership Program (Center for Substance Abuse Prevention, 1992). They suggested that 1 to 2 years are needed for the partnerships to become fully formed and functional, that is, to develop a program plan and to implement activities based on the plan. They also reported that few partnerships had reached full maturation within the first 2 years.

The most common types of partnership activities were communitywide alcohol and drug education, activities for youth, and coordination of drug prevention programs. Some partnerships worked to change law enforcement or workplace drug policies. Prevention and education were typically the partnerships' first activities. More complex activities involving legislative or policy changes came as the programs matured.

The researchers also discussed characteristics of the more advanced sites. One of the more interesting findings was that community partnership leaders were functioning at a more efficient level than leaders of grassroots partnerships. The grassroots partnerships consisted of many individuals inexperienced in the politics of community groups and service delivery systems. Process evaluators reported that the grassroots partnerships experienced serious conflict due to members feeling confused, threatened, or overwhelmed. In contrast, partnerships consisting of community leaders were more formal and bureaucratic and more experienced in formal working relationships.

Fighting Back. The evaluation of the Fighting Back programs emphasized the importance of adequate technical assistance. Technical assistance during the planning phase of the project was not readily available, however, because the funder was concerned that such assistance would give particular sites an unfair advantage in the competition to obtain an implementation grant (Klitzner et al., 1992). The lack of technical assistance resulted in several undesirable outcomes. Needs assessments were sometimes only superficial. In developing plans, site groups fell back on traditional approaches (prevention and treatment) rather than exploring public policy or other innovative approaches. Some site groups failed to

include interventions to emphasize opportunity reduction or enforcement. Others tended to reinvent the wheel in areas in which
other programs had already developed well-established and tested
protocols (e.g., physician education, adolescent assessment and
referral).

The evaluation also identified factors that helped or hindered
program development. Leadership was found to be a major deter-
minant of success. The most successful sites had a small number
of highly committed leaders who could make decisions and build
consensus. Hierarchical structures seemed to help produce success:
Small steering committees and task-specific subcommittees formed
out of the large (40- to 50-member) steering committees greatly
facilitated program development. On the other hand, greater cul-
tural diversity made consensus more difficult. Furthermore, Fighting Back programs were impeded by a declining economy. Because
the Fighting Back funds were primarily intended to coordinate and
seed services, acquisition of additional funds to provide direct
services was crucial. Although site groups were generally successful
in using the Fighting Back awards to acquire more funds, Klitzner
(personal communication, 1993) felt that they would have been
more successful under better economic conditions.

Finally, Klitzner et al. (1992) expressed concern about the ability
of the Fighting Back coalitions to sustain citizen participation—an
issue that we discussed in Chapter 3 in relation to indigenous
community antidrug initiatives. Klitzner et al. believe that the
process of competing for funding supplies a powerful motivation for
people to come together during the planning phase of the Fighting
Back project, but once the funding decisions are made, the coalitions must supply incentives and rewards to participants to maintain interest and involvement over the long run.

Weed and Seed. The process evaluation of the Weed and Seed
Initiative identifies several successes and problem areas. One of
the most significant successes, according to Roehl (1995), was
the coordination among local agencies involved in the fight against
drugs. Weed and Seed encouraged communication between federal,
state, and municipal law enforcement and other agencies and
organizations involved in local committees. Weed and Seed also

served to promote the development of community policing. It demonstrated that links between the police and the community can enhance drug enforcement efforts and began to change the image of the police among residents of the sites. Similarly, Roehl reports, Weed and Seed encouraged prosecutors to reach out and open dialogues with community groups.

Roehl (1995) also reports problems with Weed and Seed. The most significant was that the "seeding" component received so little funds that it had no chance to make a real difference. On average, sites only had a quarter of a million dollars available for seed activities, with much of that consumed by staff salaries. The impact of the few dollars available was diluted by seed committees that "were weak and in turmoil much of the time in the first project period" (Roehl, 1995, p. 10).

In some communities, the weeding initiative met with negative reactions from citizens, community groups, the media, and civil rights organizations—each concerned with possible violations of civil rights of minorities in targeted neighborhoods. Problems were evident in prosecution components as well. Roehl (1995) reports little consistency among sites in how Weed and Seed cases were prosecuted (apparently prosecutors in a number of sites handled these cases no differently from others). This inconsistency may be linked to another problem that she observed in some sites: The leading role given to U.S. attorneys sometimes led to the exclusion of local prosecutors from participation in planning and decision making in Weed and Seed.

Roehl (1995) concludes that the combined strategy of weeding and seeding is appropriate. She recommends ways to enhance the interagency cooperation vital to the programs' success and recommends that more funds be channeled to seed activities.

Profile of a Successful Program:
Hartford Areas Rally Together (HART)

In Hartford, Connecticut, the U.S. Bureau of Justice Assistance awarded a Community Responses to Drug Abuse (CRDA) Grant to the Hartford Areas Rally Together (HART) Program (Rosenbaum et al., 1992). HART, started in 1975 by a group of churches, is a coalition of six neighborhood-based organizations that have taken on a wide range of issues, including crime, affordable housing, senior citizen health care, education, unemployment, property tax relief, and zoning. The program has several paid staff as well as neighborhood volunteers who work on various projects. Each of HART's constituent organizations has a neighborhood council and a central board responsible for identifying problems and setting program priorities.

When the CRDA grant in Hartford was first implemented, HART adopted a grassroots orientation. During the second year of CRDA funding, however, a special task force was assembled to administer the CRDA demonstration. This task force (the Hartford Anti-Crime Collaborative) worked with the police department, the city manager's office, the board of education, the chamber of commerce, and various social service agencies and was involved in overall program planning, implementation, monitoring, and policy development. Most of the task force members were from existing community agencies, and they promoted an agenda that was considerably broader than HART's traditional areas of interest. Over time, community leader involvement in the collaborative dwindled, especially among ethnic minorities.

Program Activities

Cleaning Up Drug Houses. In the 3 years of Hartford's CRDA project, a wide range of social problems was addressed. An early emphasis was on closing drug houses. HART participants identified drug houses and then invited the property owners to discuss problems in these buildings. If that failed to produce results, police, housing, health, and fire departments were encouraged to inspect the buildings for code violations and mortgage holders were informed of those violations.

HART encountered many obstacles in shutting down drug houses. Prosecutors were reluctant to meet with HART members. Tenants, especially Hispanics, were afraid to report code violations for fear of eviction. City building inspectors were ineffective and inefficient. Persistence paid off, however. HART designed a database to track city inspector and law enforcement actions against problem properties. Ultimately, repairs were made to more than 20 properties targeted by HART, 5 properties were foreclosed, and several drug dealers were evicted.

Drug Treatment. In its early stages, HART became involved in assisting a local drug rehabilitation program to start an inpatient drug rehabilitation center in Hartford. The center involved area churches and two family service agencies, which became intake centers for at-risk youths referred by school officials, the criminal justice system, and the state department of youth services.

Work in the Schools. HART implemented several school activities, including a rally against drugs and antidrug assemblies. Parents lobbied school officials on issues such as classroom overcrowding, the lack of recreation programs, and drug dealing and crime around the school. As a result of HART's efforts, school officials adopted a drug education program in which 400 teachers received training in substance abuse prevention. Students were required to complete courses on the dangers of illegal drugs, and afterschool educational activities were held for at-risk youth. The programs included classes on AIDS, suicide prevention, alcoholism, leadership training, exercise, dance, cooking, and computers. Classes were organized for parents on preventing drug and gang activities, improving parenting skills, and motivating children to do well in school. Moreover, HART convinced the city to pass a drug-free school zone ordinance and 600 drug-free school zone signs were posted around schools throughout Hartford. Finally, parents successfully lobbied the school board and city council to put on the ballot a $20 million school bond for constructing a new neighborhood school. The bond issue passed during the final year of the CRDA program.

Addressing Socioeconomic Problems. As the CRDA project evolved, more attention was devoted to addressing the root causes of drugs and crime and less attention was given to law enforcement approaches. The city government was persuaded to allocate more money for summer employment programs for youth. A youth council was established to identify problems of area youth and to develop strategies for dealing with those problems. A housing fair was held to educate people about state programs to help low-income people purchase homes.

Assessing the Success
of the Hartford Experience

The CRDA project in Hartford engages in a wide and impressive array of activities to fight drugs and rebuild neighborhoods. Rosenbaum et al. (1992) reported that despite substantial efforts to mobilize residents to support the project (including mailings, phone solicitation, and door-to-door recruitment), participation was disappointingly low. This was especially true among minorities and young people. The evaluators also noted that the project lacked support among some city agencies, school officials, the police, and the courts. In spite of these shortcomings, city residents perceived that the program reduced crime, improved police responses, and increased neighborhood safety.

5. Police Antidrug Efforts

In Chapter 4, we highlighted a number of antidrug activities in areas in which community crime prevention programs had not been previously implemented or sustained. Most of the efforts were developed or administered by community organizations or private citizens with the sanctioning and support of law enforcement. In this chapter, we examine antidrug programs started by the police with the express knowledge or cooperation of neighborhood residents. We begin with an overview of police enforcement strategies against drug violations and provide an illustration from New York City of an antidrug program. We then discuss how police programs aimed at drug sales have begun to include citizen efforts. Many of the projects are part of community policing programs, which we briefly discuss and illustrate. Next, we focus on four contemporary antidrug programs that are based in police departments and have an explicit community orientation. In a section on comprehensive law enforcement approaches, we describe an innovative approach for defining and disrupting local drug markets that involves computer-mapping technologies.

Police Enforcement Strategies

Two basic police paradigms exist for combating neighborhood crime and drug problems. The first, known as the professional model, emphasizes police responsibility for order maintenance and crime control. The second, known as community policing, stresses the importance of collaboration between police and residents in the coproduction of public order and safety.

Professional policing, the dominant model of law enforcement from the early 1900s through the 1970s, transformed policing in several ways: It improved the effectiveness and efficiency of police officers by adopting technological advances in investigation, detection, and patrol; it enhanced the police image by decentralizing operations to diminish opportunities for corruption and raising standards for police hiring and promotion; and it narrowed the scope of policing by concentrating on crime-fighting activities (Kelling & Moore, 1988). Rapid responses to calls and randomized patrols in squad cars are the defining elements of the professional model (Uchida & Forst, 1994).

Community policing has become the watchword for law enforcement in the 1990s (Rosenbaum & Lurigio, 1994). Its growing popularity can be found among police administrators, politicians, and private citizens. President Clinton incorporated community policing into the Crime Bill of 1994, and proponents have heralded community policing as a revolutionary change in policing (Uchida & Forst, 1994), touting it as the "only form of policing available for anyone who seeks to improve police operations, management, or relations with the public" (Eck & Rosenbaum, 1994, p. 4).

Community policing centers around police-citizen partnerships for solving problems before they erupt into more serious incidents. It requires further decentralization of police operations, putting police officers "back on the streets." Contrasting with the professional model, community policing underscores the importance of direct engagement with citizens and flexible responses to neighborhood disorder and crime. In short, community policing necessitates changes in the fundamental philosophy of policing: from a squad patrol orientation to a foot patrol orientation; from reactive, incident-driven responses to proactive, problem-driven responses; from part-time, short-term district assignments to full-time, long-term district assignments. The purported benefits of community policing include safer neighborhoods and greater police accountability.

Professional Policing Tactics

Local police can employ several traditional enforcement tactics to control drugs at the retail or street level. One of the most popular is *buy-and-bust* (Moore, 1976), in which undercover police officers purchase drugs from street dealers and then arrest them after the transaction is completed. However, this strategy alone has not proved to be highly effective in reducing or deterring drug trafficking (e.g., Wilson, 1978). A more sophisticated variant of the technique trades the prosecution of small-time dealers for that of big-time dealers by "working up" the ladder of the drug organization (Walker, 1992). In these antidrug efforts, police often rely on informants "who know where and how drugs are bought and sold" (Kleiman, 1992, p. 144).

Since the 1980s, police departments have used retail-level enforcement strategies in massive sweeps or crackdowns, which involve greatly increased police officer presence, sanctions, and threats of apprehension (Sherman, 1990). Typically, sweeps concentrate large numbers of uniformed officers in hot spots, or known locations of heavy drug sales and use. In other words, police crackdowns are abrupt escalations in proactive enforcement activities that are intended to increase the perceived or actual threat of apprehension for certain offenses occurring in certain situations or locations. Crackdowns concentrating police resources on specific crimes in targeted areas can vary in their intensity (e.g., numbers of police personnel, arrests, raids, search warrants), tactics (e.g., buy-and-bust, observation-sale arrests), and duration (e.g., brief or sustained) (Hayeslip, 1989; Sherman, 1990; Worden, Bynum, & Frank, 1994). Worden et al. (1994) discuss the potential benefits and costs of police drug crackdowns, which are essentially refinements of older and more generic crackdown techniques:

The potential benefits of police drug crackdowns include reductions in the visibility of drug transactions, in the amount of drugs consumed, in the size of the user population, and in street crimes that are associated with drug use and drug trafficking, and improvements in the quality of life in targeted areas and in citizens' attitudes toward the police. Aside from the inescapable costs of personnel, equipment, and the benefits of foregone activities, the potential costs of drug crackdowns include increases in crime [which can result if crackdowns increase the monetary costs of drugs without reducing consumption] and in police abuse and/or subversion of their authority, and the erosion of citizen respect for and willingness to cooperate with police. (pp. 96-97)

A fundamental problem with crackdowns is the potential for trampling over the rights of innocent citizens. For example, Philadelphia's Operation Cold Turkey Program resulted in numerous arrests of innocent citizens who were "in the wrong place at the wrong time" (Pothier, 1987, p. 34). Moreover, sweeps place an inordinate strain on the criminal justice system and its resources; the spate of arrests overburdens the police, prosecutors, courts, and corrections personnel (Kleiman & Smith, 1990). In addition, Reuter et al. (1988) at the RAND Corporation found that street sweeps in Washington, D.C., from 1981 to 1986 resulted in a tenfold increase in arrests of drug dealers but did not significantly interfere with the surge in drug sales. Notwithstanding these shortcomings, Kleiman and Smith (1990) note that,

Street sweeping, if it works, serves all four goals of drug enforcement. It reduces drug abuse by reducing availability; it reduces user crime by reducing consumption without raising price; by the same token, it weakens major drug-dealing organizations by reducing the dollar value of the market; and it protects neighborhoods by reducing the flagrancy of illicit drug activity. (p. 86)

Operation Pressure Point. The most-efficient means to conduct sweeps is to concentrate on a few locations or blocks in a focused crackdown (Sherman, 1990). According to Kleiman and Smith (1990), "The ideal focused crackdown strategy in a big city would move slowly from neighborhood to neighborhood, leaving behind vigilant citizens and residual markets small enough to be controlled with residual enforcement efforts" (p. 89). A highly publicized crackdown in 1984 on the Lower East Side of New York was called Operation Pressure Point (OPP). Zimmer (1990) described and evaluated the program, which was designed to "take back the streets from drug buyers and sellers" (p. 47) in an area widely known as "a [drug] buyer's paradise" (p. 50). Regarding the ineffectiveness of the police in this neighborhood, a local drug dealer reported that,

> "There was nothing the police could do. There were more of us than there were of them and for every seller they arrested, there were ten people waiting to take his place on the street. The police were more of a nuisance than anything." (Zimmer, 1990, p. 51)

In response to intense community and police pressures, OPP began with the deployment of more than 240 additional officers to the Lower East Side. The OPP team consisted mostly of uniformed patrol officers just out of the police academy. They engaged in a variety of activities, such as dispersing crowds, making arrests, conducting drug searches, stopping and questioning individuals in known drug areas, and writing parking tickets. The police also cleared the parks and emptied abandoned buildings, which had become sites for drug use and sales. Zimmer (1990) concludes that OPP was an effective mechanism for reducing drug trafficking:

> After more than three years of Operation Pressure Point, drug trafficking became much less visible (and almost disappeared in some sections); the official crime rate declined; and people in the community began to feel more comfortable using many of the parks and public areas that were once "owned" by drug sellers, buyers, and other "undesirables." (p. 47)

Several criticisms have been leveled against the evaluation of OPP and its claims of purported success (Walker, 1992). Specifically, its program evaluation did not test for displacement effects, that is, the extent to which the drug trade and related crimes simply moved to other parts of the city. In fact, crime statistics showed that the drug problem in New York City worsened in the years following OPP. Furthermore, drug dealers appeared to adapt to the program's tactics by reducing their open dealing and paying lookouts to warn them of impending law enforcement activities. Finally, OPP was probably not cost-effective, as it required a tremendous commitment of police personnel, and it may have tacitly encouraged the police to engage in citizen harassment.

Police drug crackdowns similar to OPP have been implemented elsewhere. In Lynn, Massachusetts, a crackdown was reported to lower the volume of visible drug transactions; to increase the difficulty of obtaining drugs; and to decrease burglaries, robberies, and other crimes against persons. Problems with the evaluation of the Lynn program (i.e., the absence of a control group) make it difficult to attribute these outcomes to the crackdown. A later crackdown in Lawrence, Massachusetts, had disappointing results (Kleiman, 1988).

An evaluation of Operation Clean-Sweep in Washington, D.C., produced mixed findings (Reuter, Haaga, Murphey, & Praskac, 1988; Sherman, 1990). On the one hand, the program reportedly reduced the number of street drug markets and signs of neighborhood disorder and led to numerous arrests, prosecutions, and convictions; on the other hand, it had no effect on drug use and may have increased the incidence of violence in target areas. A crackdown in Hartford, Connecticut, had an uneven impact. In one targeted neighborhood, more than 80% of the residents reported that there was less violent crime and fewer people selling drugs after the crackdown; in the other targeted neighborhood, only 30% reported those outcomes (Caulkins, Rich, & Larson, 1991).

Community-Police
Drug Enforcement Programs

In 1987, Oakland, California, and Birmingham, Alabama, were sites for studies on the effectiveness of different police strategies to control street drug trafficking. The U.S. Bureau of Justice Assistance (BJA) funded antidrug programs in both cities and the National

Institute of Justice (NIJ) funded Police Foundation evaluations of
the programs. The lead researchers on the project were Uchida,
Forst, and Annan (see Uchida, Forst, & Annan, 1992).

BJA selected Birmingham and Oakland because they were moderately large cities with definitive plans to implement police enforcement strategies against drugs. In addition, their racial compo-
sitions were fairly evenly distributed between African Americans
and whites and they each employed about 600 police officers. The
two cities differed in several important ways. Oakland's crime rates
and drug problems were among the worst in the country whereas
Birmingham's crime and drug problems were only moderately
serious for a large city. Although cocaine was prevalent in both
cities, Oakland's drug problem involved crack. In contrast, Birmingham had a more serious problem with powder cocaine and with
Dilaudid, a synthetic form of heroin. Essentially, the cities were
paired to yield a more robust and broader evaluation of police
antidrug efforts.

Oakland. Oakland's attempt to combat drug-related crime consisted of two major activities: the police department's Special Duty
Unit 3 (SDU-3) and door-to-door interviews with residents. SDU-3's
responsibility was to provide high-visibility drug enforcement and
to use buy-and-bust operations to disrupt street-level dealing. High-
visibility drug enforcement involved uniformed SDU-3 officers
working in teams of two to patrol areas in two targeted beats. These
officers initiated encounters with citizens: stopping motor vehicles
and bicycle riders, questioning persons who appeared to be engaged
in drug activities, stopping and frisking suspicious individuals, and
discussing neighborhood problems with residents. The fundamental difference between SDU-3 officers and routine patrol officers was
that the special unit officers were highly proactive in their activities;
instead of waiting for citizens to call for police assistance or services,
the SDU-3 officers took the first step in making contacts with
people on the street.

In the two targeted beats, buy-and-bust operations were concentrated in areas of heavy drug trafficking, or hot spots. The buy team
was staffed by two undercover officers who rode around in incon-
spicuous cars and bought drugs from dealers in a variety of locations

in residential areas, for example, on street corners and in front of motels, houses, and local stores. The bust team stayed within striking distance of the sellers and were clearly identified as police officers. They wore bullet-proof vests, drove semimarked police cars, and were in continuous contact with one another on handheld radios.

The buy team located drug sellers, informed the bust team of their location, and made deals with the sellers. After a deal was completed, the buy team would notify the bust team, which quickly arrived on the scene to arrest the dealers. The bust team would also arrest any buyers who were in the vicinity of the incident.

In the early months of the program, SDU-3 officers were very successful in making arrests and in causing drug dealers to move to other locations and to conceal their drugs in nearby hideouts rather than on their persons. The drug dealers soon began to recognize members of the teams by sight and by name, however, which obviously compromised their effectiveness as law enforcement agents and placed their personal safety in jeopardy. To counter this development, the team introduced a variety of different vehicles and officers. The unit also began to rely more on drug informants, or "snitches," to keep them abreast of new drug locations and traffickers.

To complement these undercover operations, the Oakland Police Department added a community-oriented component to its overall drug enforcement effort. This part of the city's initiative was implemented in two other beats and largely involved citizen contact through two mechanisms: door-to-door interviews and a drug hotline. The contacts were designed to inform citizens of the department's antidrug activities and to educate them regarding the signs of drug trafficking and the various ways they could assist the police to combat drugs, such as calling the drug hotline with useful information about drug trafficking and drug dealers. During contacts, the police assured citizens who provided them with drug leads that their anonymity would be protected and the information they volunteered would remain strictly confidential. Moreover, the police conducted interviews with residents and distributed pamphlets describing the drug hotline. The interviews asked citizens about the condition of their neighborhoods, the most important problems in their neighborhoods, and their opinions concerning ways to alleviate those problems. Overall, the police completed nearly 1,900 interviews in the two beats. More than half of the citizen respondents mentioned drugs as the most important problem in their community.

The evaluation of Oakland's program used a before-after design and was conducted in three phases. In Phase 1 (3 months in duration), evaluators gathered baseline data prior to implementation of the program; they administered citizen interviews, collected police crime statistics, and performed observations of police activity in four randomly chosen beats throughout the city. Researchers chose these beats so that they could evaluate the impact of each component of the program alone and in combination. In Phase 2 (6 months in duration), the program became operational: Beat 25 received the SDU-3 intervention, Beat 7 received door-to-door intervention alone, Beat 34 received the combination of interventions, and Beat 11 received only routine police services and served as the control beat. In Phase 3 (6 months in duration), the interventions were rotated: Beat 25 became the control site, Beat 34 became the SDU-3 site, Beat 11 became the door-to-door site, and Beat 7 became the combination site. Evaluators collected data at the end of Phase 2 and of Phase 3 and compared those findings to the baseline measures.

According to Uchida et al. (1992), the Oakland program had several favorable impacts on residents and crime:

- Residents in all three types of intervention beats felt safer after the interventions than before.
- Residents perceived that the police's ability to combat drugs had improved in the beats that received SDU-3 enforcement alone.
- Residents were more satisfied with the way in which the police handled neighborhood problems in the beat that received door-to-door contacts.
- In the SDU-3 beat only, residents perceived that the incidence of vandalism of cars decreased; in the door-to-door beat only, they perceived that the incidence of sexual assaults decreased.
- Residents perceived that the incidence of drug trafficking had decreased in the SDU-3 beat, the door-to-door beat, and the combination beat.

- Declines in reported violent crime were found in the door-to-door beat and in the combination beat. The SDU-3 beat experienced reductions in violent crimes and burglaries, but not in robberies. The door-to-door beat experienced reductions in violent crimes, but not in burglaries. In the combination beat, burglaries increased 5% compared to a citywide increase of 11%.

Birmingham. The Birmingham Police Department's antidrug program was similar to Oakland's; Birmingham also used a combination of law enforcement and community-oriented policing tactics. As its law enforcement component, the department implemented an operation called Caine Break (CB) in select areas of the city. CB was conducted in two stages: a "straight-buy" approach that targeted sellers and a sting approach that targeted buyers. In Stage 1, officers in unmarked vans, which were equipped with audiovisual recording technology, bought drugs from dealers on street corners and in front of homes in residential neighborhoods. Each interaction was secretly recorded. Other officers were part of a backup team that monitored the activities of the buy team via radio contact and was prepared to intervene if problems ensued. Stage 1 operations lasted approximately 4 months and culminated several months later "when arrest warrants were served on the sellers en masse" (Uchida et al., 1992, p. 35).

The second stage of CB involved new legislation in Alabama that upgraded "solicitation for the purposes of purchasing drugs" from a misdemeanor to a felony. In this stage, narcotics detectives posed as street-corner drug dealers and waited for potential buyers to approach them. A surveillance van and two marked cars were positioned near the sales locations. The officers posing as drug dealers asked potential buyers to name their desired drug and to show cash for its purchase. The presentation of money consummated the deal and satisfied the state law governing drug conspiracy. The police recorded all interactions on audiotape and videotape. Stage 2 of CB also culminated in mass arrests (i.e., "large scale bust-outs") several months after the sting operation.

Like Oakland's program, Birmingham's drug enforcement effort included a community policing component. The community-based initiative was modeled after community policing programs in Houston and Newark and concentrated on door-to-door contacts with citizens. During contacts, police informed citizens about department antidrug activities; distributed pamphlets on crime prevention; and surveyed residents about neighborhood crime, drug trafficking, and other neighborhood problems.

Finally, the department opened a police substation in a housing development where a rash of drug-related shootings had occurred. The substation was a fully secured apartment where police were assigned 24 hours a day.

Three experimental beats were involved in the evaluation of Birmingham's program: Goldwire received Operation CB, Gate City received door-to-door police-citizen contacts, and Kingston received the police substation. Residents of these beats were interviewed before and 9 months after the interventions were implemented. The survey was designed to measure changes in citizens' perceptions regarding drugs, quality-of-life issues, crime, police services, and safety from crime. In addition, police crime statistics were analyzed before, during, and after the experimental period. The primary findings of Uchida et al.'s (1992) evaluation were as follows:

- Operation CB in Goldwire was successful with regard to drug arrests and favorable press coverage and also had a positive impact on property crime.
- Residents in Kingston, where the substation was opened, reported greater satisfaction with the police on a number of dimensions (e.g., police success in working with residents and maintaining order in the neighborhood) and perceived a reduction in auto thefts.
- Residents in Gate City, where door-to-door contacts were implemented, reported that the police were more sensitive to their concerns and were more visible in the neighborhood. Significant reductions were evident in reported homicides, rape, assaults, and robberies.
- Residents in none of the experimental beats changed in their perceptions of the drug problem.

Philadelphia. During the mid-1980s, Philadelphia experienced major increases in violent and serious crimes, especially those associated with drug trafficking and use. At that time, citywide crime statistics indicated that nearly 30% of homicides were drug related and that narcotics arrests were the second-highest crime category among all offenses. In December 1987, the commanding officer of the South Division of the Philadelphia Police Department announced that the police would attempt to forge an active partnership with community residents to identify and solve drug and crime problems in the Queen Village neighborhood, which had endured a variety of difficulties linked to crime and drugs. The plan for enhanced police-community interaction was called Project DOE, which referred to the specific patrol sectors (D, O, and E) where the program was implemented (Greene & McLaughlin, 1993).

Project DOE was grounded in the basic tenets of community policing, which suggest that the police should work proactively with citizens to address the underlying forces that create neighborhood disruption and disintegration (Goldstein, 1990; Skogan, 1990). According to the basic principles of community policing, the police should cultivate a cooperative, problem-solving relationship with residents to coproduce community safety and solidarity (Eck & Spelman, 1987; Skolnik & Bayley, 1986). In accordance with the community policing model, Project DOE had four features (Greene & McLaughlin, 1993): *community stability*, which involved opening a police ministation to increase police visibility and responsiveness; *community activation*, which involved providing citizens with information about neighborhood drug problems, discussing with citizens ways to solve these problems, and helping citizens to develop neighborhood organizations; *directed patrol activities*, which involved using crime analysis to focus police efforts in areas of Queen Village with the highest levels of crime, drugs, and disorder; and *enhanced service delivery*, which involved convening a service team of public and private agencies to facilitate the coordination of services for the neighborhood.

Greene and McLaughlin (1993) offer four valuable lessons for police officials interested in replicating the police-community partnership of Project DOE. First, police officers should be thoroughly trained in their new, collaborative roles. The officers in Project DOE were well trained in the traditional functions of the police, but they did not have enough experience in being "problem solvers" and "community activists."

Second, community-oriented drug programs in law enforcement may engender conflict between program officers and other police personnel working in and around a project's area. Such programs may represent interests that diverge from the larger interests of the department. In Philadelphia, Project DOE was not readily accepted by all members of the police department and became a flash point for the divisive issue of police centralization. Greene and McLaughlin (1993) recommend more structured and monitored interactions between program and nonprogram officers, and activities to help officers understand the changing expectations of police performance that police-community partnerships engender.

Third, neighborhood residents must also be prepared to adjust to basic changes in police-community relations. As Greene and McLaughlin (1993) note,

> The DOE Project may have underestimated the need for "training the community" for its own self-defense. Systematic training for the community might have increased DOE impacts, while quickening community confidence and the building of relationships among neighbors. (p. 159)

Finally, the DOE Project underscored how difficult it is for the police to unify the interests and efforts of diverse neighborhoods and to coordinate and integrate service delivery.

New York City. The New York City Police Department (NYPD) implemented its Tactical Narcotics Team (TNT) approach in 1988 in the borough of Queens; by fall 1989, the program was expanded to Manhattan and Brooklyn. The TNT drug enforcement strategy emphasized quick buy-and-busts and high police visibility in identified hot spots. A novel aspect of the strategy was the team's mobility—a TNT remained in a target area no longer than 90 days. The itinerant nature of the program was useful in three respects: It maximized resources by shifting the team around a borough to meet the needs of several communities per year; it reduced the likelihood that undercover officers would be recognized by local drug traffickers; and it ensured that operations would not yield diminishing returns if the program only displaced, but did not eradicate, drug activity. During the first 90 days of operations, in the 67th and 70th precincts in Queens, TNTs made 1,011 and 560 arrests, respectively (Sadd & Grinc, 1993). Sviridoff and Hillsman (1994) report that there are currently seven TNTs (one in each of New York City's police patrol boroughs) and that, in 1990, TNTs produced more than 24,000 narcotics arrests—two thirds of which were for felonies.

The TNT program was designed to include an active community orientation. According to Sadd and Grinc (1993) of the Vera Institute, who studied the program, the NYPD expected that,

> TNT will reduce the effects of drug trafficking on the quality of life in the target area, help community residents reclaim streets and parks, bring businesses back to the community, and reduce the level of fear among those who live and work in the area. (p. 180)

The community became involved in the program primarily through a series of meetings held at the beginning, middle, and end of the TNT period in a precinct, which lasted approximately 3 months. During these meetings, community leaders, local politicians, and representatives of city agencies were told about the nature and accomplishments of the program, were persuaded to support the initiative, were encouraged to call the Drugbusters hotline to provide information regarding drug activities, and were asked to give feedback on how they thought the TNT was performing in their neighborhood.

Sadd and Grinc (1993) used several methods to evaluate the impact of TNTs, including extensive interviews with residents, community leaders, and businesspersons in each target area. These surveys were conducted in two experimental areas in Queens (67th and 70th precincts) and one comparison area (71st precinct). The experimental areas' data were collected prior to program implementation, at the end of the 90-day period, and 3 months after the TNTs left the areas. The purpose of the interviews was "to measure changes in respondents' perceptions or behavior as a result of TNT's intervention in the community" (p. 183).

The evaluation showed that the TNT impact was very limited. Most community leaders believed that the program had an immediate effect on drugs and supported its goals and presence, but they thought the impact was transient—after a TNT left an area, drug trafficking returned to its previous level.

The residents of the experimental areas also perceived the program to be ineffective against drug trafficking: In both the before and after surveys, residents thought that drug use and sales were a "big" problem in their neighborhood.

Similarly, the TNT program appeared to have no effects on public perceptions of crime, the quality of life in the community, or police-community relations. Moreover, the program seemed to increase fear of crime for a small percentage of residents who indicated that the TNT chased drug dealers from the streets into the hallways of their apartment buildings. In the words of a respondent from the 67th precinct,

> "Yeah, drug dealing has changed. It was heavy in the streets. But TNT has busted a lot of those people and now they are back in the apartment buildings and they are back in my hallways. Before TNT came, they were pushing heavy on the street or in front of the building, now they are in the building." (Sadd & Grinc, 1993, p. 190)

According to Sadd and Grinc (1993), survey respondents attributed the apparent failure of the TNT approach to five factors: the short duration of operations (3 months); lenient sentences for drug dealers; racial and ethnic conflicts in neighborhoods, which preclude residents from organizing; residents' fear of retaliation from drug dealers for cooperating with the police; and the overriding influence of larger social problems, which prevent enforcement tactics alone from successfully combating drugs.

Sviridoff and Hillsman (1994), however, indicate that the TNT program did have positive effects on the drug market. It virtually shut down street-level drug dealing on one block in a target location, and overall drug trafficking on the streets became less visible, especially in areas that were "geographically separate from highly concentrated drug markets, and in areas that catered to purchasers from outside the neighborhood" (p. 121).

Comprehensive Law
Enforcement Approaches

Most recently, the federal government has funded law enforcement agencies in several cities to implement comprehensive approaches to neighborhood drug enforcement. These strategies combine community policing with civil enforcement measures—use of code enforcement and drug house abatement statutes. The guiding philosophy behind comprehensive approaches is problem-oriented policing (Eck & Spelman, 1987; Goldstein, 1990). Police officers work with community representatives to define problems of concern to area residents and develop plans to solve them. The solutions can include implementing traditional law enforcement responses, soliciting cooperation of other municipal agencies, enforcing civil statutes on code violations or drug house abatement, licensing of liquor establishments, or making changes in the physical environment to make spaces more defensible (Newman, 1973). The first example of the comprehensive approach to neighborhood drug enforcement that we discuss is the Drug Market Analysis Project (DMAP) in Hartford, Connecticut; Pittsburgh, Pennsylvania; Kansas City, Missouri; Jersey City, New Jersey; and San Diego, California. The other is the Oakland, California, Specialized Multi-Agency Response Team (SMART).

Drug Market Analysis Project. The Justice Department recently funded an innovative experiment in five cities to define and disrupt local drug markets by employing computer-based technologies. A consortium of researchers assessed the effectiveness of this effort, known as the Drug Market Analysis Project (DMAP).

DMAP is based on previous research analyzing the geographic origins of police calls for service in Minneapolis (Sherman et al., 1989), which suggested that a disproportionate share of crimes occur at a small number of locations. Sherman et al. (1989) argued for proactive intervention at these locations, or hot spots.

DMAP expands the notion of hot spots from a discrete street address to larger areas—drug markets that encompass a block or contiguous string of blocks (Weisburd & Green, 1994). Drug markets are defined by the presence of distributors or large-scale suppliers;

mid-level dealers who stock local retailers; retail dealers who sell drugs to users; and freelance operators who deal drugs irregularly and are often users themselves (Taxman & McEwen, 1994).

Computer-mapping techniques play a key role in most of the DMAP sites. Data on drug activity from various sources (calls for service, arrests, citizen tips) are fed into a computer. The computer's information systems collate the information and produce pin maps highlighting hot spots. The systems are also capable of providing details for each hot spot, such as the types of drugs sold, hours of drug sales, and characteristics of arrestees (Taxman & McEwen, 1994; Weisburd & Green, 1994).

The information developed by the DMAP databases assists law enforcement officials in selecting appropriate methods to shut down particular drug markets. For example, if a computer database indicates that a specific individual sells drugs from several locations, the seller may be part of a "Speakeasy" market, which is not place specific and requires buyers to supply a password to initiate transactions. Law enforcement officials can then concentrate on working with informants to discover the password, which will lead to undercover buy-and-busts (Taxman & McEwen, 1994).

Capitalizing on the new computer information, law enforcement strategies were formulated and implemented in five sites:

Hartford. Law enforcement officials implemented a program of highly visible uniform patrols. Raids, buy-and-bust operations, and reverse stings were also used (Tien, Rich, Shell, Larson, & Donnelly, 1993).

Pittsburgh. Police relied heavily on reverse stings and buy-and-bust operations.

Kansas City. Heavily armed police initiated a series of highly visible raids on crack houses, battering down doors and sometimes using explosives to gain entry.

Jersey City. Officials employed multiple strategies, including drug abatement statutes, code enforcement, enhanced uniformed patrol, undercover surveillance, and crackdowns.

San Diego. Law enforcement agencies combined traditional narcotics enforcement efforts with problem-oriented approaches.

DMAP promises to expand our knowledge about how drug markets operate and how they can be curtailed. For example, DMAP data are showing that drug markets differ in the types of drugs available, hours of operations, and types of locations from which sales occur (Weisburd & Green, 1994). There are indications that within a given market these features may vary over time as the market changes (Rengert, 1990).

DMAP appears to be yielding useful insights into how police can tailor strategies to particular drug markets. Early evaluations from the DMAP sites confirm that certain law enforcement strategies work better in some types of drug markets than in others. For example, the reverse stings used in Pittsburgh proved to be a valuable tool with bazaar-style drug markets in which buyers and sellers did not know each other (Taxman & McEwen, 1994). They clearly would not have worked in markets with more restricted access. In Hartford, enhanced patrol and vehicle safety checks were most effective in a market confined to a small area with clear physical boundaries (Tien & Rich, 1994). In Jersey City, a randomized experiment assigned matched pairs of hot spots to receive standard or enhanced law enforcement. In the enhanced condition, police initiated crackdowns, sought to engage business owners and citizens in crime control efforts, and aggressively pursued enforcement of municipal codes. These efforts led to a significant decline in narcotics complaints and arrests in the experimental areas (Weisburd & Green, 1995).

Oakland's SMART Program. Oakland's Specialized Multi-Agency Response Team (SMART) program adopted a problem-solving approach to neighborhood drug enforcement that emphasizes working relationships between police and citizens, property owners, and business proprietors. Although SMART uses traditional law enforcement methods, the program targets drug hot spots and uses building code violations and abatement statutes to clean up problem locations. Civil code enforcement improves the physical appearance of problem locations and creates an environment in which people are less able or willing to engage in deviant activity (Green, 1996).

Police officers coordinate inspections of drug nuisances with representatives from the city's fire, housing, public works, and vector control departments. On average, 70% of problem locations are cited for at least one code violation. SMART officers work with property owners to clear up code violations, evict problem tenants, and make environmental alterations. These civil actions are complemented by arrests of drug dealers.

Green (1996) reported that SMART was quite successful in reducing drug and crime problems in targeted areas. SMART sites experienced increased citizen reporting of drug problems, fewer arrests, and fewer field contacts relative to citywide trends. Before-and-after photos showed improvements in the appearance of SMART sites after the intervention. Green also concluded that code violations combined with traditional enforcement tactics resulted in improvements, especially at commercial and owner-occupied properties.

Profile of a Successful Program: Hartford's COMPASS Program

In 1990, the Hartford, Connecticut, Police Department (HPD) started the Cartographic Oriented Management Program for the Abatement of Street Sales (COMPASS). COMPASS employed a reclamation and stabilization approach based on the "weed and seed" model for improving neighborhoods; it was located in areas of the city where crime and drug sales were rampant. For the weeding component of the program, the police used computer-based mapping to perform a drug-market analysis, and they engaged in community policing and other antidrug strategies. For the seeding component of the program, the police attempted to form partnerships with the community for the purpose of replacing drug businesses and activities with legitimate enterprises.

HPD chose the COMPASS target areas on the basis of their serious drug problems, which included outdoor drug sales, and their levels of community organizing, which would become instrumental during the seeding efforts of the program. As Tien et al. (1993) noted, "The target areas had to have active and well-organized community groups to facilitate defining the needs and setting the priorities" (pp. 13-14). In addition, target locations were assigned a community service officer (CSO). Program oversight became the responsibility of the Reclamation Steering Committee, which had four goals: to reduce the incidence of drug-related crimes, to empower residents to take control of their own neighborhoods, to increase residents' ability to become economically self-sufficient, and to enable service providers and residents to collaborate.

Weeding began with HPD's execution of arrest warrants for persons involved in the area's drug trade and the deployment of the Crime Suppression Unit (CSU). CSU officers, freed from calls for routine services, engaged full-time in foot patrols, vehicle safety checks, and buy-and-bust operations. Seeding activities were designed to include HPD, residents, community groups, and institutions. CSOs served as mediators between HPD and city agencies and between target area residents and businesses, institutions, and organizations. The reclamation and stabilization approach began when,

> The police reclaimed a target area, first by performing a drug market analysis . . . and then by employing a variety of high visibility and antidrug tactics over a several month period. Once an area is reclaimed, the stabilization phase of the COMPASS program attempts to maintain the area in its reclaimed state over the long term through a partnership involving the community, the city, and the police. (Tien et al., 1993, p. vii)

To identify drug-market areas, COMPASS used several sources of information, such as drug arrests, hotline complaints, drug overdose calls for service, loitering calls for service, and gun calls for service. Tien et al. (1993) also observed that "perceptions of police officers, citizens, arrestees, drug users, and other knowledgeable persons about the level of drug activity in an area are useful measures [for identifying drug markets]" (pp. 3-4). In the first 2 years of the program, COMPASS was implemented in four target areas with distinctive characteristics:

Charter Oak Terrace—a small, geographically isolated area of public housing buildings surrounded by a river, a railroad, and an interstate

highway. In the 3 months before COMPASS, police had made drug
arrests at 12 locations.

Milner—a 16-block area with a mix of multifamily apartment buildings
and houses. In the 3 months before COMPASS, police had made
drug arrests at 36 locations.

Frog Hollow—located near a congested commercial street and encompass-
ing an area three times as large as Milner and six times as large as
Charter Oak Terrace. In the 3 months before COMPASS, police had
made drug arrests at more than 60 locations.

Asylum Hill—a diverse residential-commercial neighborhood nearly the
size of Frog Hollow but with one third as many residents. In the 3
months before COMPASS, police had made arrests at 28 locations.

To assess the impact of COMPASS in these locations, four sets
of evaluation measures were used: input, process, outcome, and
systemic. Data were collected through police records, surveys, interviews with program participants, and on-site monitoring. Based
on experiences in the four COMPASS target areas, Tien and Rich
(1994) reached the following conclusions:

- COMPASS generated a lot of favorable publicity for the city and HPD,
  which increased program support in the target areas. Knowing the
  locations of the CSU helped drug dealers and their customers adapt
  their behaviors, however, and may have lessened the effectiveness of
  weeding efforts.

- Geography is an important feature of weeding tactics. Well-defined
  boundaries define target areas for police interventions and a limited
  number of roads into and out of a target area help police to restrict
  access to locations.

- Weeding success encourages community participation in subsequent
  seeding activities. When community involvement is active and visible,
  both weeding and seeding efforts are more successful.

- Turmoil in city government and budgetary restrictions impeded the
  implementation of the seeding component of COMPASS. COMPASS
  became primarily a police-only weeding program, but it had a positive
  impact on some of the poorest areas of the community as indicated by
  changes in residents' perceptions about violent crime and drug sales
  and reductions in reported crimes.

6. Drug House Abatement Programs

Drug dealers often operate from indoor locations. They work out of their own homes or apartments or take over an entire building in a public housing development. In other instances, they occupy one of the many abandoned buildings in low-income, inner-city neighborhoods. Sometimes, the locations become sites for both drug sales and use: "Crack houses" and "shooting galleries" are locations where drugs can be bought and used on the premises.

Anyone who tries to keep dealers from using these locations— including neighbors who complain about the street disorder and crime associated with the drug trade or landowners who complain about drug dealers and customers on their properties—may become targets of threats or retaliation. Police may be called on to curtail drug sales, but their effectiveness is limited. In optimal circumstances, careful undercover work may culminate in an arrest, but arrested dealers are often released on bail or sentenced to probation, which allows them to continue plying their trade. Moreover, the police do not have the resources to continually monitor problem addresses. When police "take the heat off," chances are the drug dealing will resume as usual.

People unlucky enough to live near drug houses seldom have the luxury of simply escaping the problem. The best they can hope for is to move to a neighborhood in a part of town without the same intensity of drug and crime problems. In the late 1980s, people discovered a promising tool for getting rid of drug dealers. In fact, it may be the most effective strategy that police or citizens can use to combat neighborhood drug problems. This tool applies nuisance abatement ordinances to close down or confiscate properties that are sites for drug sales. In this chapter, we discuss drug house abatement programs, their impacts, and their implications for drug enforcement.

Portland, Oregon, was a leader in using civil abatement laws. During the mid-1980s, staff of Portland Office of Neighborhood Associations organized citizens' efforts to track and report drug activity. The staff developed a special reporting form to provide the police with highly detailed information on neighborhood drug transactions—detailed enough to enable police to acquire search warrants and raid individual locations. Office staff also organized residents to survey, for code violations, buildings where drug sales transpired. They lobbied the police and district attorney for increased patrols and investigations of drug activity. In 1987, they helped to enact a municipal drug house ordinance enabling the city to impose civil penalties on the owners of properties used for drug dealing. In just the first month of the ordinance, city officials brought 12 civil suits against property owners and contacted 30 more for possible action.

Pursuing property owners as an antidrug strategy was a revolutionary approach. For the first time, rather than going directly after drug dealers, officials put the responsibility for dealers' actions on the owners of properties where the dealers conducted business. Portland property owners could curb their tenants' behavior any way they saw fit: They could warn tenants, ask them to get rid of unwanted houseguests, or install better security systems. But officials expected that property owners would evict the drug dealers, which could possibly help rid the neighborhood of the problem. The new ordinance and the city's warning letters gave the landowners the ammunition they needed to win eviction orders in housing court.

The approach was also revolutionary in being based on civil rather than criminal law. Instead of needing to prove beyond a reasonable doubt that a crime had been committed, officials now only had to demonstrate that a drug nuisance existed, by virtue of an arrest, seizure of drugs or drug paraphernalia, or a successful undercover buy at the location.

Encouraged by the successes of civil abatement efforts in Portland, Denver and several other pioneering cities and states around the country began to adopt existing nuisance legislation to combat drugs. By 1992, an American Bar Association (ABA) study found that 24 states had passed statutes specifically designed to control drug activity on private property (Smith et al., 1992). In some cases, these statutes updated old "bawdy house" laws designed to curb prostitution. Most states authorize preliminary injunctions requiring that the premises be immediately vacated on filing of civil actions. Judges can issue permanent injunctions after civil hearings. The most common sanction is closing properties for up to one year. In practice, such orders are frequently stayed if the owner posts a cash or property bond. In some states, buildings may be sold at auction with the proceeds going to state or local government.

Abatement programs are similar to the asset forfeiture programs that state and federal governments operate under statutory provisions that authorize government agencies to seize and sell property involved in illegal activity. Proceeds from these sales often go directly to the agency initiating the forfeiture action. Forfeiture is used more sparingly than abatement. In most instances, abatement is more appropriate, because the state's aim is usually to correct a problem through threat of closure or confiscation, not to deprive owners of their property. In addition, the kinds of properties that the state targets for abatement are seldom (by virtue of their locations and conditions) valuable enough to justify the expense of a forfeiture action.

Varieties of Abatement Programs

A wide range of abatement programs exist. Most are run by district or city attorneys and police departments and operate without any special funding. Some programs target hundreds of properties each year, others just a few. Two dimensions distinguish these programs from one another. The first is whether the community plays a significant role in deciding which properties to target. The second is whether officials attempt to abate drug nuisances by warning property owners or by immediately filing suit against them.

Project Dunamis in Dayton, Ohio, is an example of intense community involvement in abatement efforts. The program, started by a church group, takes advantage of an existing state law that defines a dwelling as a nuisance if activities there are "obnoxious or offensive" or endanger the health and safety of others. A unique aspect of Project Dunamis is that citizens themselves file civil lawsuits claiming drug houses are a nuisance. Program organizers propagated the strategy by training citizens in other Dayton neighborhoods and in other cities across the state.

At the other extreme, the Cook County, Illinois, abatement program, run by the state attorney's office, has relatively little direct community involvement. Program representatives attend meetings of community groups to solicit cooperation from citizens, but an evaluation of the program showed that just 1 in 10 properties were targeted from citizen complaints. The bulk came from the police and from criminal prosecutions filed by the state attorney's office (Lurigio et al., 1993).

In most programs, abatement efforts are initiated with a letter to a property owner describing the drug nuisance and the consequences of allowing it to continue. This first warning is usually enough to motivate the owner to take action. In programs in which warning letters are issued, civil suits are seldom required to induce compliance. For example, Smith et al. (1992) report that civil suits were filed in less than 5% of abatement actions taken in Alexandria, Virginia, and Milwaukee, Wisconsin. In Cook County, the rate of civil or housing court filings was also less than 5% (Lurigio et al., 1993).

Other programs operate under a different philosophy. Officials in the abatement programs in Toledo, Ohio, and Houston, Texas, do not warn property owners; instead, they immediately file civil suits. In Houston, officials request a hearing to obtain a temporary injunction. Property owners are notified of the hearing date and are given an opportunity to keep their buildings open if they post cash bonds and agree to permanent injunctions.

Toledo's program is even more severe. After program staff identify an abatement target, prosecutors seek a temporary restraining order against the property. The order allows the building to be closed and padlocked immediately, and without notice to the owner, on the grounds that irreparable harm is being done to the community. On the same day that the court issues the order, a multiagency team of 25 persons, equipped with battering rams and search warrants, executes the order. The temporary restraining order remains in effect for 2 weeks pending a hearing for a preliminary or permanent injunction, after which the building may be closed for one year.

Needless to say, this approach was not well received by Toledo property owners. Moreover, in padlocking a building for a year in a marginal area, there is a risk that the property will be vandalized, abandoned, and will never re-enter the rental housing market. Over time, prosecutors have softened their approach by permitting "innocent" owners to post bonds and keep their properties open.

Effectiveness of Abatement Programs

Abatement programs that rely primarily on warning letters are a low-cost and potentially effective weapon in the war on illegal drugs. Both the ABA (Smith et al., 1992) and Loyola University of Chicago (Lurigio et al., 1993) recently studied the effectiveness of these programs by addressing three issues: First, they examined whether the programs had really abated drug nuisances. Second, they assessed the impact of abatement actions on the quality of life in a neighborhood as judged through the eyes of neighborhood residents. Third, they explored whether abatement actions actually reduced drug dealing or simply displaced it to another neighborhood. The ABA study included abatement programs in five cities (Milwaukee, Houston, Toledo, San Francisco, and Alexandria); the Loyola University study focused on a single program in Cook County (Chicago).

Abatement Success. Results of both studies indicate that abatement programs are quite effective in achieving their immediate goal of eradicating drug activity. In all six cities, program records showed that compliance was obtained from the owner or no further problems were experienced on the premises in at least 85% of the targeted properties. In the great majority of cases, compliance was obtained through evictions of problem tenants.

Of course, program records on compliance are only as valid as the thoroughness of follow-up investigations. Follow-up is normally a police function (following a request by the city or county attorney), and thoroughness varied widely across programs. In a majority of the programs, no police personnel were dedicated to this activity, so follow-up was done when time permitted or not at all. In Cook County, follow-up consisted mostly of a request for police information on new arrests at targeted addresses.

The fact that follow-up was not done systematically raises the question of whether program abatement successes, as based on case files, are in fact as high as the ABA and Loyola studies report. One exception in this regard is the Milwaukee program, which included scrupulous follow-up. Plainclothes detectives routinely attempt to make undercover buys at targeted locations approximately 75 days following the initial abatement letters. Milwaukee case files indicate continued or renewed drug activity at the 75-day follow-up in just 8% of cases (Smith et al., 1992). If Milwaukee's success can be generalized to other programs, then abatement efforts appear to be very effective.

The ABA and Loyola studies also investigated program impact on the quality of life in neighborhoods. In the ABA study, investigators conducted interviews with 300 residents living in the vicinity of properties that the abatement programs had targeted in the five participating cities. Respondents were asked about their knowledge of the local abatement program, their support of its goals, their awareness of abatement targets in their neighborhoods, and their perceptions of changes in the quality of neighborhood life since the abatement occurred.

The ABA study reports that abatement actions were highly visible. Approximately half of the residents surveyed across the five cities were aware of the abatement actions. Community awareness was highest in cities where officials padlocked properties and publicized their efforts through the media. Awareness was lowest in cities in which the abatement action usually consisted of a letter followed by the quiet eviction of a problem tenant.

Community support for drug abatement was overwhelming: More than 90% of the total number of residents surveyed were greatly in favor of it. Given this level of citizen support, program officials should publicize their activities to communicate that local government cares and to instill public confidence that drug problems can be effectively controlled. This conclusion is supported by the finding that 7 in 10 respondents across the five cities reported that the abatement action had empowered them to fight drugs in their community.

There is also evidence that the abatement efforts reduced signs of neighborhood disorder. One in three respondents believed that the actions had reduced drug sales on their block, and one in four believed that the actions had reduced crime in general. A similar proportion believed that the problems of public drinking and adolescents hanging out on the street had been reduced as a result of the abatement actions.

Although abatement efforts had positive effects on residents' perceptions of disorder, they did not affect their perceptions of quality of life. Some respondents (about one in five) reported that their neighborhood had become safer since the abatement actions, but roughly the same proportion believed that their neighborhood had become less safe. Similarly, about one in five respondents liked their neighborhood more and one in five liked it less since the abatement actions. Negative changes in perceptions of the quality of neighborhood life may have occurred because the abatement actions alerted residents (for the first time) that serious drug problems existed in their neighborhood. Researchers have reported similar effects in studies of burglary prevention programs (e.g., Rosenbaum, 1983; Winkel, 1987).

The positive changes in residents' perceptions of crime and disorder observed in the ABA study are questionable because researchers did not include comparison measures—they did not assess residents' perceptions before the abatement actions occurred or compare the perceptions of residents in areas in which abatements occurred to those of residents in other, similar neighborhoods where no abatements occurred.

The Loyola University investigation of abatement in Cook County eliminated these shortcomings. In that study, residents were interviewed on 20 blocks where abatements had occurred and on 20 similar blocks nearby where no abatements had occurred. The results obtained with this more rigorous methodology are less optimistic than the conclusions of the ABA researchers. Less than one in five residents on blocks where the program had targeted properties was aware of the abatement. Moreover, residents on targeted blocks were no more likely than residents on nontargeted blocks to perceive improvements in drug activity, disorder, or safety on the block.

In contrast, the majority of community leaders and police personnel surveyed in the Loyola study believed that the program resulted in visible changes in their community and that the program was an important part of their community's efforts to reduce drug activity. An ethnographic study conducted as part of the Loyola evaluation confirmed that program actions had visible effects on the community. Based on observations at nearly all of the locations, buildings that had been the targets of abatements showed no obvious drug activity.

What explains the discrepancy between residents' perceptions and those of community leaders, police, and ethnographers? The Loyola study probably failed to find an impact on residents' perceptions because the program in question operates quietly with staff working with property owners and not seeking extensive media coverage of abatement actions. Residents' awareness of Cook County's abatement actions was much lower than resident awareness in the cities surveyed in the ABA study. Abatement programs that use public displays of force and seek media attention are likely to have the greatest effect on residents' perceptions of drug activity and disorder.

Abatement programs appear to be quite successful in abating drug problems and changing residents' perceptions of crime and disorder. The larger question is whether an abatement action diminishes a drug dealer's activity or merely displaces it to another location. Proponents of abatement programs argue that forcing drug dealers to move impedes their business because they lose customers or are forced to compete with established dealers in new locations. One

Milwaukee attorney, who has defended property owners in abatement suits, has likened abatement actions to " 'scattering rats in a woodpile' " (Smith et al., 1992, p. 26). He contends that it is better for the police to know where the dealers work, whether concentrated in particular buildings or neighborhoods, as opposed to dispersing them throughout the city in unknown locations.

Because Milwaukee's abatement program targets properties in only one area of the city, the ABA researchers were able to analyze data from the Milwaukee Police Department to test for displacement effects. Comparing the first 4 months of 1990 and 1991, they found that total reported crime had declined in the abatement area by 21% whereas citywide crime had declined by only 14% over the same period. This difference was statistically significant. During the same time interval, crime in the census tracts surrounding the abatement area declined by exactly the same amount as citywide crime. Therefore, no evidence was found to suggest that crime was simply displaced from the target area to surrounding areas.

The Loyola researchers followed a small sample of abatement program evictees. Using local probation records, the evictees were tracked to new addresses. With a police computer, investigators checked arrests at those new locations. They found that no arrests had occurred at any of the locations since the dealers had moved there. Interviews with neighbors at those locations strongly suggested that drug sales were continuing in two of the four cases, however. These limited findings indicate that evicted drug dealers may not stay as active (or as open) at their new residences, although some individuals clearly continue to sell drugs. Such changes in behavior may be most likely for marginal dealers—those who have been termed "opportunists" (Buerger, 1992) or "occasional" sellers (Reuter et al., 1990). Persons who sell small quantities of drugs to supplement their income are the most likely to be dissuaded when the costs of their illegal activity are raised.

A much larger and more systematic investigation of drug dealers evicted through drug house abatement was conducted by the Milwaukee Police Department (1994). Detectives randomly sampled 100 cases (involving 201 individuals) that had been assigned to drug abatement personnel. Detectives used all investigative means at their disposal to locate individuals who had been involved in the sale or manufacture of drugs and who had been investigated and displaced by the drug abatement program.

The detectives were successful in locating 97% of the individuals in the sample. Among those located, 25% were incarcerated in federal, state, or local institutions, 7% had moved from the jurisdiction, and 2% were deceased. For those tracked to new locations within Milwaukee, detectives checked drug complaints at the new addresses and attempted undercover drug buys. They found that 12% of the entire sample, or 19% of those found and still at liberty to sell drugs, remained in the drug business. The results were so striking that the Milwaukee Police Department discontinued the pilot tracking program, deciding it was unnecessary and clearly not worth the cost of the continuing investigations. They had answered to their satisfaction the question of whether abatement programs actually *discouraged* drug sellers over an extended period of time or simply *deterred* them for a short while (Green, 1996).

The Question of Fairness

Although research findings suggest that abatement efforts can work, program administrators should be cognizant of the consequences of abatement actions on people's lives. In cases in which someone has already been prosecuted for drug dealing, an eviction resulting from an abatement action could be characterized as an additional punishment for the crime. This concern is especially relevant in Cook County, where more than half of all program cases were drawn from drug prosecutions of the state attorney's office. Although drug dealers may be undesirable tenants, their rights still need to be protected. A drug nuisance abatement ordinance in Trenton, New Jersey, was struck down by the state supreme court on the grounds that its eviction provisions violated protections under the state's tenants' rights legislation.

Probably of more concern to most people are the rights of innocent parties affected by abatement actions. What about the family members evicted with drug dealers? Should parents, spouses, children, and other dependents suffer possible homelessness because of the wrongdoings of a family member? What about innocent people thrown out of their home when an entire apartment building is closed? In cities where civil suits are filed without prior warning to landowners, such outcomes are not unusual.

Property owners and their attorneys have maintained that it is unfair for the state to shift the burden of enforcing drug laws from law enforcement agencies to private citizens. In their view, property owners should not be responsible for correcting society's problems, nor should their properties or safety be exposed to the risks that often accompany eviction actions against drug dealers. It has also been argued, in several hard-fought suits in Milwaukee, that drug house abatement laws violate owners' rights to due process and equal protection, and deprive property owners of rightful income without offering any just compensation.

In a small survey conducted as part of the ABA abatement study, property owners were given a chance to express their opinions about abatement programs. Only 7 of the 20 respondents reported that they thought the law was a bad idea. Most seemed just as anxious as city officials to eliminate drug sales from their properties, and many believed that abatement laws work. Half of the respondents who had evicted tenants reported that drug problems, loitering, and graffiti had been reduced as a result of the abatement action. About half of those surveyed also stated that the experience had made them change their management practices or the way they screened prospective tenants.

Only 8 landlords agreed that the law was fair to property owners. Half of the respondents cited the costs they were sometimes forced to bear as a result of abatement actions. For example, one owner paid $5,000 in legal fees and another reported $45,000 in lost income as a result of his property being padlocked. Several mentioned acts of retaliation by persons threatened with eviction, including the beating of a property manager and shots fired through a window of a targeted building. One third of the landowners reported that innocent people, most often children, were forced to move as a result of eviction actions.

What property owners felt was most unfair was the way in which the abatement laws were exercised. Many owners felt that they were being treated as criminals. The court suits and sternly worded warning letters especially rankled owners (half of the sample) who themselves had alerted the police to the drug problem. In addition, the government's adversarial position was resented by those owners who stated that they had been unaware of drug problems on their properties prior to the abatement actions. Many respondents stated that they would have been happy to cooperate with authorities had they been approached in a reasonable manner. Nonetheless, even when property owners cooperate, their response may not go far enough to satisfy city officials.

Surveyed property owners in the ABA study were also asked whether their experience with the abatement program had discouraged them from owning rental properties in the future. One third of them answered yes, although several attributed their decisions to deteriorating neighborhoods and crime.

Findings from the Loyola evaluation, based on a much larger sample of property owners, confirmed the ABA results. Similar to property owners in the cities that the ABA researchers studied, Cook County owners held mixed views about abatement programs. Most did not like the idea of holding property owners responsible for drug dealing in their buildings; two out of three owners reported that they were unaware that problems even existed prior to the abatement actions. And most property owners reported that the abatement process was costly. Two out of three reported costs stemming from lost rent or from court fees to evict drug dealers. One in four reported property damage or threats made against them by dealers, including a handful who were actually assaulted. But most Cook County property owners believed that the abatement program staff had treated them fairly. Finally, four out of five believed that the abatement had reduced drug dealing and other signs of disorder at their properties.

Some Concerns and Some Solutions

The evidence from both major studies of drug house abatement programs strongly indicates that the programs are very effective in ridding buildings of drug nuisances. The cost to public agencies of the programs is minimal: Most abatements are achieved just for the cost of a letter. In fact, many cities conduct drug nuisance abatement activities with funds from existing municipal budgets.

Serious concerns about abatement programs need to be addressed, however. Programs should include procedures to minimize the number of innocent parties evicted as a result of abatement actions and to resettle innocent parties who are evicted. Abatement program staff often take the position that they are not responsible for innocent persons dislocated by their actions (although, informally, they often assist in relocation). The use of court suits and building closures as a last, rather than a first, resort would help to reduce the number of innocent parties evicted.

Initial reliance on warning letters instead of court actions would also alleviate other concerns about abatement programs. Minimizing the padlocking of buildings would lessen the likelihood that targeted properties will be abandoned. Targeted buildings are typically in poor condition and are located in deteriorating neighborhoods. Closing them for an extended period invites vandalism and deprives owners of rental income necessary to cover mortgage payments. Furthermore, filing court suits without prior warning to property owners unnecessarily alienates them. Few owners want drug dealers on their premises, because such tenants tend to be destructive and to drive off respectable tenants. Treating property owners as potential allies makes much better sense than making them enemies by initiating court suits.

Another way to increase the cooperation of property owners is for abatement program staff to sponsor workshops to inform owners about their responsibilities under abatement laws. In addition, staff can provide owners with suggestions on screening prospective tenants and improving security.

A final concern about abatement programs is whether they reduce drug sales or merely move them to another neighborhood. To be fair, abatement program staff only claim to ameliorate a situation at a particular location. But it would be hard to justify the time and money spent on such programs if all they accomplish is to move dealers around. Overall, evidence suggests that abatement actions may actually reduce, not just displace, drug sales. More careful, sophisticated research is needed to determine the effects of abatement programs on drug dealers' careers.

Profile of a Successful Program:
Milwaukee's Drug Abatement Team

Milwaukee's drug abatement program is a well-organized and aggressive effort to rid problem locations of drug dealing. It is also well financed, receiving $500,000 in state funds on July 1, 1990, which was the official start date of the program. In the program's first 18 months, more than 450 properties were targeted by the city Drug Abatement Team, an interagency task force consisting of police, staff of the city attorney's office, building inspectors, and members of community organizations. Nearly 9 in 10 property owners notified about a nuisance have abated the problems without need for the city to file civil suits.

How the Team Began. Milwaukee's West Side is predominantly African American and residential, with a mix of single-family homes, duplexes, and large apartment complexes. During the early 1980s, Milwaukee suffered a serious economic slump caused by the loss of manufacturing jobs, which had traditionally been the basis of the city's economy. Later in the decade, the city pulled itself out of the slump by making old manufacturing plants more efficient and creating jobs in the service sector. But even as the rest of the city boomed, unemployment in the African American community remained consistently high at approximately 20%. Drug use and violence soared: Homicides doubled in just 3 years between 1988 and 1990.

The Drug Abatement Team was formed out of the efforts of a state representative and the Cooperation West Side Association (COWSA), a well-established community association experienced in anticrime activities. The team persuaded the legislature to pass a drug abatement statute. The new law is an updated version of an older bawdy house law that allows a civil suit to be filed to declare a property a public nuisance. If the circuit court finds that a property is being used to facilitate the delivery or manufacture of drugs, it may issue injunctive relief. An order to close can follow and, eventually, an order to sell, with the owner getting nothing from the proceeds. A property owner can submit an undertaking to the court to attempt to stop the process. If the court closes a property, the structure must remain closed until any building code violations are cleared.

How the Team Operates. Properties are targeted by the Drug Abatement Team following complaints from community residents or tips from police informants; each of these methods of identifying problem properties accounts for about half of the team's work. COWSA gathers community complaints about drug nuisances through a special hotline. COWSA staff filter the information from the calls (i.e., drug sale locations are tracked and reports of drug use are screened out) and fax it to the police detectives assigned to the Drug Abatement Team. Most callers prefer to remain anonymous, and they are not pressed to divulge their name. The police communicate with COWSA on actions taken against reported problem locations; callers can get updates on their cases by calling the hotline 3 to 4 weeks after their initial reports.

After a drug sale location is reported to the police, detectives survey the property and attempt to conduct an undercover buy-and-bust. If police recover drugs on properties or make arrests for drug dealing, they send property owners an abatement letter, which informs them that drug activity has been documented at a particular address (specific apartments are not named in multiunit buildings). Owners are given 5 days to stop the activity. If they do not, the property may be declared a public nuisance and may be closed or sold. Owners are encouraged to call the detectives assigned to the Drug Abatement Team for assistance.

During this interim period, police continue to monitor complaints from neighbors and within 2 weeks they attempt another buy at the location. If the detectives are unsuccessful, they follow up a second time, 60 days later, to ensure that the nuisance has been abated.

If drug sales persist, a second letter is sent. If this letter fails to abate the nuisance, the Milwaukee city attorney is brought into the process. A staff attorney prepares a civil suit, which can eventually result in the closure or sale of the property. Simultaneously, the city attorney may call in a building inspector to look for code violations.

The owner must correct violations or face the imposition of a fine through municipal court.

In the event that the court orders a property to be sold, revenues generated from the sale are used to recoup expenses of the Drug Abatement Team and to compensate the mortgage holder. Any surplus revenue goes to law enforcement agencies, to drug and alcohol treatment programs, and to programs for housing rehabilitation and crime control. The property owner receives none of the proceeds.

In the vast majority of cases, city officials claim that the initial letter alone is sufficient to abate the problem. That view is substantiated by police department statistics, which indicate that more than 9 in 10 abatement actions are cleared by compliance, nearly all through evictions of problem tenants by landlords. (Clearance is defined as cessation of drug activity at a location. Detectives on the Drug Abatement Team decide what action the property owner must take to abate the problem.)

Only 5% of abatement cases are referred to the city attorney for possible civil action. Most of these cases are resolved through negotiation with the owners. Only a handful of suits are filed—all cases in which property owners are clearly unresponsive.

Several suits have been hard fought and prominent in the press. The most notorious case was against the owner of a 36-unit building. Members of the Drug Abatement Team characterized the building as the worst drug-dealing location on the West Side. In the 2 years prior to the team's action against the property, police had made 164 arrests at the apartment house, resulting in 354 criminal charges. The building has been described as "being to drugs what McDonald's is to hamburgers." A police detective stated, " 'If this new law doesn't work for this building it won't work. Might as well pack up and go home' " (Smith et al., 1992, p. 21).

The building's appearance was deceptive. It was relatively new and well kept, built originally for young, white-collar workers interested in living near downtown jobs. Over time, however, its residents became transients. According to the police, as many as 10 units were involved in drug trafficking. The building acquired a reputation as a great place for drug dealers to do business. But not all of the residents were drug dealers and some had lived in the building for a dozen years.

City officials claimed that the owner of the building did little to abate drug sales at the property. Detectives assigned to the Drug Abatement Team found that drug sales remained flagrant. In fact, after the city had targeted the property, the building manager was shot to death while he slept in his apartment in what police characterized as a drug-related shooting.

The building owner asserted that he did attempt to bring the property into compliance. He claimed to have evicted several tenants, to have cooperated with the police by reporting drug activity and providing keys to the building, to have corrected more than 60 building code violations noted by the Drug Abatement Team's building inspector, and to have improved security. City officials did not dispute his claims but believed that the owner's actions did not go far enough, given the scope of the problem. The city attorney demanded that the building be cleared out and closed for 60 to 90 days.

The owner refused, and the city filed suit in circuit court. The owner then filed a countersuit challenging the city's right to take over his property. The suit alleged that the owner's rights to equal protection and due process were violated, and that the city could not deprive him of his property without compensation. Before the suit was brought to a conclusion, the property burned.

Effects on the Community. A sample of 50 cases taken from program files showed that the Drug Abatement Team primarily targeted small- to medium-sized rental complexes (Smith et al., 1992). The majority of the cases (70%) in the sample were resolved by removing one or more problem tenants. Among the locations initially cleared, only 8% showed new signs of drug activity when detectives checked them 60 days later. Thus, the team's successes seem to be long lasting.

The local newspapers were replete with examples of blocks being cleaned up through the efforts of the Drug Abatement Team, which ensued after calls to 911 and arrests failed to stop drug sales at those problem locations. Probably the biggest changes were documented in the area around 27th and Wells streets, where the Drug Abatement Team cleared entire apartment buildings. Residents nearby reported that not only drug sales but also prostitution and use of firearms declined dramatically. City officials hope that as blocks are cleared of dealers, banks may be more willing to provide mortgage money and to invest in redevelopment projects on Milwaukee's West Side.

7. Conclusion

The Success of Neighborhood Antidrug Programs

Neighborhood efforts to combat drug dealing can be quite effective. When properly implemented, they directly influence the nonmonetary costs of drug use, that is, the time it takes customers to find drugs for sale and their risk of being arrested for buying and possessing drugs. Thus, the overall cost of obtaining drugs is increased whereas their monetary cost is not (the latter may encourage more drug-related crime). Neighborhood drug enforcement weakens drug organizations by reducing the dollar value of the market and strengthens communities by reducing blatant drug dealing and use.

We have seen that police efforts *can* reduce visible neighborhood drug selling. Most research on police crackdowns suggests that they do disrupt local drug markets. It is unclear whether crackdowns are effective in all types of neighborhoods and against all types of drug markets. There are suggestions that they work better against bazaar-type markets than market types where business is conducted between acquaintances. Moreover, crackdowns appear to have only a temporary effect, which leads to the question whether their high monetary costs are worth the short-term gain.

In many ways, community policing seems to be a better law enforcement approach to neighborhood drug problems than traditional police methods. Rather than alienate large parts of the community through roughshod tactics, community policing recruits community members into the struggle to preserve and protect the neighborhood. Evaluation data suggests that community policing methods applied against drug selling can lead to resident perceptions of decreased drug activity and crime *and* more favorable perceptions of the police.

From data we reviewed in Chapter 6, we believe that drug house abatement laws are probably the most cost-effective law enforcement approach to combating neighborhood drug problems. Many cities conduct drug nuisance abatement activities with funds from existing municipal budgets. Similar to other local antidrug initiatives, abatement actions are popular with residents of neighborhoods where drug dealing is extensive (Rosenbaum, 1993).

Abatement actions appear to be remarkably effective in cleaning up problem buildings and reducing signs of disorder in the vicinity of targeted properties. Aggressive abatement actions have been teamed with traditional law enforcement approaches to produce dramatic changes in recalcitrant drug markets in Minneapolis (Buerger, 1992) and in Oakland (Green, 1996). Evidence to date suggests that the problems tend not to return any time soon and generally are not displaced to other locations.

But as we said at the outset of this book, law enforcement agencies are only half of the picture when it comes to neighborhood antidrug efforts. Citizen involvement is critical. The research we reviewed suggests that police sweeps can have a lasting impact only when combined with efforts to recruit residents to assist in preventing drug dealers from returning to the neighborhood through patrols, block watch programs, or other means. Likewise, drug house abatement programs can operate successfully only when they work hand in hand with community anticrime groups that provide information about drug hot spots. The primary goal of community policing is to mobilize citizens to work in partnership with the police. Citizens can act as the eyes and ears of law enforcement through block watch programs and can discourage drug dealers from conducting business through highly visible neighborhood patrols.

Police sweeps, community policing, drug house abatement efforts, and citizen antidrug programs all can reduce the frequency of visible drug activity in a neighborhood. We believe that the success of neighborhood antidrug initiatives—in contrast to earlier citizens' attempts to combat street crimes and burglaries—hinges on the fact that selling drugs is a retail business. Drug sellers are attached to locations in a way that creates a vulnerability not experienced by robbers, rapists, or burglars, who can strike anywhere in a neighborhood. Because drug dealers are conducting a business, the places and times they work must be fairly consistent. Customers must be able to locate them and make purchases with a relatively low risk of arrest. Police and community groups can use dealers' need for a stable business environment to discourage drug sales. Forcing dealers to stay on the move increases search time for potential customers and may frustrate marginal dealers. Increasing the discomfort level of potential customers (by increasing their risk of arrest, harassing them, or exposing them to public scrutiny) may also discourage some drug users.

According to routine activity theory (e.g., Clarke & Felson, 1993; Cohen & Felson, 1979), crime occurs when a motivated offender and a suitable target (victim) come together in the absence of a capable guardian. This theory has gained wide acceptance in the criminal justice community because it provides a framework for understanding crimes involving victims (e.g., Fattah, 1991, 1993). It does not apply, however, at least in its original form, for place-based victimless crimes such as drug dealing or prostitution. The two entities that must converge for a drug sale or successful sex solicitation to occur are a motivated offender and a suitable *customer*, rather than a victim.

When applied to drug sales, routine activity theory can be modified as follows: A drug transaction will occur when a motivated seller and a suitable buyer come together in the absence of a capable guardian. Neighborhood antidrug enforcement works by providing capable guardians in the form of increased police presence, citizen patrols, citizen block watch, and so forth. The guardians can be few in number and particularly effective exactly because they have a good idea where to find place-based retail drug sellers. Other neighborhood antidrug efforts work by removing sellers (buy-and-bust operations) or buyers (reverse stings) from the equation or making it harder for the two to come together (evictions stemming from drug house abatement activities or police crackdowns).

Pitfalls for Neighborhood Antidrug Efforts

Displacement. Neighborhood drug enforcement programs are not without pitfalls. Drug dealers driven from one neighborhood by zealous citizens or police may simply set up shop somewhere else. Lab (1992) reviewed evidence concerning the displacement of crime (primarily robbery and burglary) caused by citizen prevention programs and concluded that "displacement is a plausible concern in considering the impact of the [crime prevention] projects" (p. 81). Because drug dealing is more like a business than robbing or breaking and entering, we might expect drug dealers to be especially recalcitrant: Chased from one location, they may have strong financial incentives to establish themselves elsewhere.

Evaluations of neighborhood antidrug efforts have seldom found displacement effects, however. For example, displacement has been found only in a few studies of police crackdowns (see Sherman, 1990). The research on drug house abatement we reviewed in Chapter 6 gives little indication that displacement occurs when drug dealers are dislocated. Green (1996) reported that not only did Oakland's project SMART fail to generate displacement effects, but it diffused benefits to the surrounding area, confirming a phenomenon observed earlier by Clarke and Weisburd (1994). In other words, drug problems improved at targeted sites and in the area surrounding each individual SMART site. More research is needed to determine the extent to which community antidrug efforts displace problems or diffuse benefits.

Even if displacement is found to occur, Barr and Pease (1990) argue that when drug activity travels from high- to low-crime areas, it has "benign" consequences because it evens out the geographic distribution of crime. Moreover, if motivated citizens' neighborhoods are able to displace crime to neighborhoods with less-motivated residents, that could be regarded as a fair outcome. Maybe an increase in crime in a less-organized neighborhood will lead citizens there to become more organized. These are important policy questions.

Consequences of Arrest. The aggressive police pursuit of neighborhood drug dealers produces large numbers of arrestees that the courts are not equipped to handle. Drug arrests in the United States increased 52% between 1980 and 1987, whereas the total number of arrests for nondrug cases increased by just 11% (Belenko, 1993). Drug arrests currently number in excess of one million each year. Some have wondered whether attention to enforcement of drug-related laws may be diverting money and resources away from enforcing other laws (Blumstein, 1993). Others argue that strict enforcement of drug-related laws is a sensible strategy for reducing all types of crime, as drug offenders commit a large proportion of all crimes (e.g., Boyum & Kleiman, 1995).

The large increases in drug arrests have placed a tremendous strain on the courts and corrections facilities. Case-processing time for drug felonies has risen precipitously—in some cities up to a year (Goerdt & Martin, 1989). When the courts become overwhelmed with drug cases, they typically respond by releasing defendants on a wholesale basis. For example, Press (1987) reports that a police crackdown in New York City drug markets between 1985 and 1987 resulted in a large backlog of pending cases: The combination of crowded court dockets and crowded jails put pressure on courts to plea-bargain cases "cheaply," in effect neutralizing the value of mass arrests. Similarly, Smith et al. (1992) found that dramatic increases in drug case backlogs in Chicago preceded an increase in the use of nonreporting probation as a sentencing option.

The increase in drug arrests has seriously affected a whole generation of African American youth who are, in disproportionate numbers, caught by the police in drug crackdowns and other enforcement efforts (Tonry, 1994). Tonry demonstrates that drug arrests have been responsible for worsening racial disparities in prisons across the country.

Erosion of Civil Liberties. In the aggressive pursuit of neighborhood drug enforcement, police should guard against the erosion of individual constitutional rights. Drug crackdowns often involve stop-and-frisk practices. Historically, the courts have permitted the police to use this tactic when they suspected the presence of weapons or potential for violence. But it is certainly questionable whether transporting illegal drugs from one location to another constitutes a similar immediate danger (Rosenbaum, 1993).

A recent spate of antiloitering laws has been passed in an attempt to make it easier for police to curb neighborhood drug sales. These laws have sometimes been directed against drug-dealing gangs by authorizing police to disperse groups of known gang members. Other times, they have restricted loitering in certain areas labeled as high-drug-activity locations (Davis, Smith, Lurigio, & Skogan, 1991).

Stop-and-frisk practices and antiloitering laws are cause for concern because they infringe on the rights of individuals for the greater welfare of the community. They are also troublesome because they are used disproportionately against minorities. According to Rosenbaum (1993), "This approach to the drug war is likely to encourage prejudicial responses that are unfavorable to disadvantaged and minority communities, whereby skin color is too often associated with drug activity" (p. 68). One consequence of the unequal application of stop-and-frisk practices and antiloitering ordinances has been heightened tensions between police and minority youth.

Aggressive neighborhood drug enforcement that produces a large number of arrests may lead to a short-circuiting of due process rights for the accused. Numerous urban courts have adopted measures to shorten the time from arrest to disposition, including dedicating entire courtrooms to drug caseloads in the hope that specialization will produce speedier justice. But speedier justice may result in poorer-quality justice. Smith, Lurigio, Davis, Goretsky-Elstein, and Popkin (1994) reported that in one jurisdiction with special drug courtrooms, some court officials expressed concern that they were dispensing "assembly line" justice: In fact, the researchers found that the rate of dispositions by trial had declined (guilty pleas went up) and the proportion of defendants represented by private attorneys had decreased since the special courtrooms opened.

Drug house abatement and forfeiture laws may also erode civil liberties, especially when recklessly applied. Because abatement strategies hold property owners accountable for tenants' behaviors, these statutes may infringe on owners' rights to use and enjoy property (Smith et al., 1992). Furthermore, statutes that permit authorities to close properties without notifying owners may infringe on due process rights. Abatement laws may be unfair to targeted tenants because they require a lower standard of proof of drug dealing than do criminal statutes. Finally, improperly applied abatement laws can injure innocent family members who are evicted with drug dealers as well as other tenants who are forced out with the closure of entire buildings.

Asset forfeiture laws have generated far more debate about civil liberties than abatement statutes because they ignore the fundamental presumption of innocence: Under many forfeiture statutes, authorities can seize property prior to trial, even if the owner is unaware that the property was used to store or distribute drugs (Rosenbaum, 1993). To obtain their seized property, defendants must prove that they are innocent or that their property was not used for drug activity. Fortunately, asset forfeiture laws are not used nearly as often as abatement laws because real estate values in poor neighborhoods do not justify the expense of the process.

Regardless of these constitutional issues, residents living in neighborhoods with a lot of drug sales want aggressive law enforcement. Rosenbaum (1993) found that most residents of inner-city neighborhoods were willing to accept infringements on individual rights (e.g., rounding up suspected drug users even without sufficient evidence) to reduce drug trafficking. He concludes that "residents of neighborhoods with visible drug markets have repeatedly called for police crackdowns on their own neighbors and their calls have been heard" (p. 77).

Addressing the Roots of the Drug Problem

Ultimately, to be successful, efforts to curb drug use and sales must address the social problems that underlie these activities (Chavis, Speer, Resnick, & Zippay, 1993). Researchers have identified a host of factors that increase the likelihood of drug or alcohol abuse. Risk of abuse is higher in neighborhoods where people are economically deprived, where indicators of social and physical disorder are prevalent, and where community sentiment generally allows drug abuse and other illicit activities (e.g., Fagan, 1988; Krosnick & Judd, 1986). Drug and alcohol abuse are associated with family characteristics such as intrafamily conflict, inconsistent parental discipline, poor communication, and drug use by parents or siblings (e.g., Penning & Barnes, 1982). Psychological factors can also explain drug and alcohol abuse (e.g., sensation seeking and low impulse control) (Shedler & Block, 1990).

Law enforcement approaches to curbing illegal drugs are not designed to ameliorate the severe economic distress, lack of community and family cohesion, and low levels of personal control that contribute to drug abuse. Addressing these problems is a complex, monumental undertaking that requires a comprehensive planning strategy, which, so far, this country has refused to pursue.

Drug abuse can be overcome with the proper measures. Interventions that have shown promise include early childhood and family support programs, parenting-skills training, social skills training, and programs to enhance academic achievement (e.g., Baum & Forehand, 1981; Hawkins & Lam, 1987; Horacek, Ramey, Campbell, Hoffman, & Fletcher, 1987).

True solutions to the problem of drug abuse must address the breakdown of communities and families that are at the root cause of drug abuse. But according to Chavis et al. (1993), the institutions that can help to address these problems have become detached from the communities they serve. To ensure that institutions are accountable and responsive to the community, Chavis et al. argue that citizens need to have a closer relationship with institutions. That is where voluntary organizations, such as neighborhood associations, block associations, youth organizations, and church groups, have an important role to play. These organizations let citizens "gain control of their community and seek accountability . . . of the larger institutions" (Chavis et al., 1993, p. 261).

Churches are in the forefront of the struggle to reduce factors that contribute to drug abuse. Churches often organize antidrug vigils and marches. They play an important role in developing youth programs and other efforts to ameliorate the causes of drug abuse. Schools have begun to play an important role as well, through drug education programs and programs to involve families and the community at large in the success of students (Sizer, 1992). Through the sorts of community policing programs we discussed in Chapter 5, police departments also have become involved in rebuilding neighborhoods to provide a decent quality of life and discourage drug abuse.

Chavis et al. (1993) propose a three-tiered approach to "rebuilding community capacity to address drug abuse" (p. 251). According to the model, social planners work to rebuild links between the management of institutions that serve the community, grassroots organizations, and residents. The first tier in their model consists of *citywide partnership leaders* (e.g., mayor, police chief, church leaders, etc.). These leaders form *partnership committees*—the second tier of the model. These committees are working groups of staff from the offices represented by the partnership leaders. The committees provide program ideas and respond to *neighborhood coalitions*, the third tier of the model. The neighborhood coalitions consist of leaders of grassroots community organizations (e.g., block associations), each with a significant constituency in the neighborhood. These coalitions assess community needs and work with the partnership committees to solve problems.

This model has been put into practice in several New Jersey cities. In Newark, for example, a partnership was formed consisting of nearly 100 institutions. The partnership has designed and implemented family support centers, started a community development corporation, and promoted community policing. In Patterson, the partnership has conducted several neighborhood health fairs, sponsored antidrug rallies, and created a "health industry enterprise zone" to attract health-related jobs to the community. It also has initiated a pilot community policing program. In each of the cities where partnerships have been formed, the key has been to build the "mutual accountability of institutions at all levels in the city to begin to mobilize on behalf of the interest of the whole community" (Chavis et al., 1993, p. 279).

Achieving large-scale reductions in the sale and use of illegal drugs is an enormous undertaking. When we realize that the drug problem is embedded in a host of social ills that are tied to the breakdown of the social fabric of inner-city communities, the challenge becomes especially daunting. It is not that we do not know how to rebuild these communities; the question is whether we have the desire and are willing to commit the resources necessary to do the job.

We pay for our collective failure to act in a variety of ways. The problems of inner cities are not contained within the boundaries of deteriorated neighborhoods. The social problems of dysfunctional urban neighborhoods result in billions of dollars spent on income assistance programs, criminal justice services, health services, and social programs. We lose our competitive edge as a nation by having a large segment of the workforce with minimal skills. We pay as well through heightened fear of crime—worry over having our property taken or our person violated. And we pay a moral cost, knowing that we can make a difference, but choosing instead to ignore urban problems. Ultimately, it is less costly to respond to the needs of our cities than to look the other way.

References

Anglin, M. D., & Hser, Y. (1990). Treatment of drug abuse. In M. Tonry & J. Q. Wilson (Eds.), *Drugs and crime* (pp. 398-460). Chicago: University of Chicago Press.

Anglin, M. D., & Speckart, G. (1988). Narcotics use and crime: A multisample, multimethod analysis. *Criminology, 26*, 197-231.

Ball, J. C., Rosen, L., Flueck, J. A., & Nurco, D. N. (1981). The criminality of heroin addicts: When addicted and when off opiates. In J. A. Inciardi (Ed.), *Drugs crime connection* (pp. 39-65). Beverly Hills, CA: Sage.

Barr, R., & Pease, K. (1990). A place for every crime and every crime in its place: An alternative perspective on crime displacement. In D. Evans, N. Fife, & D. Herbert (Eds.), *Crime, policing, and place: Essays in environmental criminology* (pp. 277-318). London: Routledge.

Baum, C., & Forehand, R. (1981). Long-term follow-up assessment of parent training by use of multiple outcome measures. *Behavior Therapy, 12*, 643-652.

Belenko, S. (1993). *Crack and the evolution of anti-drug policy*. Westport, CT: Greenwood.

Bickman, L., Lavrakas, P. J., & Green, S. K. (1977). *National Evaluation Program—Phase I summary report: Citizen crime reporting projects*. Washington, DC: Law Enforcement Assistance Administration.

Bickman, L., & Rosenbaum, D. (1977). Crime reporting as a function of bystander encouragement, surveillance, and credibility. *Journal of Personality and Social Psychology, 35*, 577-586.

Blumstein, A. (1993). Making rationality relevant: The American Society of Criminology 1992 Presidential Address. *Criminology, 31*, 1-16.

Boyum, D., & Kleiman, M. A. R. (1995). Alcohol and other drugs. In J. Q. Wilson & J. Petersilia (Eds.), *Crime* (pp. 295-326). San Francisco: ICS Press.

133

Brown, G., & Silverman, L. (1974). The retail price of heroin: Estimation and applications. *Journal of the American Statistical Association, 347*, 595-606.

Buerger, M. (1992). Defensive strategies of the street-level drug trade. *Journal of Crime and Justice, 15*, 31-51.

Caulkins, J. P., Rich, T. C., & Larson, R. C. (1991). *Geography's impact on the success of focused local drug enforcement operations or "crackdowns."* Unpublished manuscript.

Center for Substance Abuse Prevention. (1992). *National evaluation of the community partnership Demonstration Program.* Washington, DC: U.S. Department of Health and Human Services.

Chaiken, J. M., & Chaiken, M. (1982). *Varieties of criminal behavior.* Santa Monica, CA: RAND.

Chaiken, M. R. (1986). Crime rates and substance abuse among types of offenders. In B. D. Johnson & E. Wish (Eds.), *Crime rates among drug-abusing offenders* (Final report to the National Institute of Justice, pp. 47-68).

Chavis, D., Speer, P., Resnick, I., & Zippay, A. (1993). Building community capacity to address alcohol and drug abuse: Getting to the heart of the problem. In R. C. Davis, A. Lurigio, & D. Rosenbaum (Eds.), *Drugs and the community* (pp. 251-284). Springfield, IL: Charles C Thomas.

Chavis, D. M., & Wandersman, A. (1990). Sense of community in the urban environment: A catalyst for participation and community development. *American Journal of Community Psychology, 18*, 55-81.

Cheh, M. (1991). Constitutional limits on using civil remedies to achieve criminal law objectives: Understanding and transcending the criminal-civil law distinction. *Hastings Law Journal, 42*, 1325-1413.

Clarke, R. V. (Ed.). (1992). *Situational crime prevention: Successful case studies.* New York: Harrow & Heston.

Clarke, R. V., & Felson, M. (1993). Introduction: Criminology, routine activity, and rational choice. In R. V. Clarke & M. Felson (Eds.), *Routine activity and rational choice* (pp. 1-16). New Brunswick, NJ: Transaction Books.

Clarke, R. V., & Weisburd, D. (1994). Diffusion of crime control benefits: Observations on the reverse of displacement. In R. V. Clarke (Ed.), *Crime prevention series* (No. 2, pp. 165-184). Monsey, NY: Criminal Justice Press.

Clayton, R. R. (1981). Federal drugs-crime research: Setting the agenda. In J. Inciardi (Ed.), *The drugs-crime connection* (pp. 35-51). Beverly Hills, CA: Sage.

Cohen, L. E., & Felson, M. (1979). Social change and crime rate trends: A routine activity theory approach. *American Sociological Review, 44*, 588-608.

Conklin, J. (1975). *The impact of crime.* New York: Macmillan.

Cook, R., & Roehl, J. (1993). National evaluation of the community partnership program: Preliminary findings. In R. C. Davis, A. Lurigio, & D. Rosenbaum (Eds.), *Drugs and the community* (pp. 225-250). Springfield, IL: Charles C Thomas.

Cook, T. D., & Campbell, D. T. (1979). *Quasi-experimentation: Design and analysis issues for field settings.* Chicago: Rand McNally.

Cornish, D. B., & Clarke, R. R. (Eds.). (1986). *The reasoning criminal.* New York: Springer-Verlag.

Courtwright, D. (1986). *Dark paradise.* Cambridge, MA: Harvard University Press.

Davis, R. C. (1989). *Community response to crack.* Grant proposal of Victim Services Agency, New York, to the National Institute of Justice.

Davis, R. C., Smith, B. E., & Hillenbrand, S. W. (1991). *Reporting of drug-related crimes: Resident and police perspectives.* Washington, DC: American Bar Association.

Davis, R. C., Smith, B. E., Lurigio, A. J., & Skogan, W. G. (1991). *Community response to crack: Grassroots anti-drug programs.* Report of the Victim Services Agency, New York, to the National Institute of Justice.

Decker, S. (1993, October). *Slinging dope: The role of gangs and gang members in drug sales.* Paper presented at the annual meeting of the Midwest Criminal Justice Association, Chicago.

DuBow, F., & Emmons, D. (1981). The community hypothesis. In D. A. Lewis (Ed.), *Reactions to crime* (pp. 167-182). Beverly Hills, CA: Sage.

Eck, J. E. (1994, November). *The segmented model: Strategies for understanding and defining drug markets.* Paper presented at the annual meeting of the American Society for Criminology, Miami, FL.

Eck, J. E., & Rosenbaum, D. P. (1994). The new police order: Effectiveness, equity, and efficiency in community policing. In D. P. Rosenbaum (Ed.), *The challenge of community policing: Testing the promises* (pp. 3-23). Thousand Oaks, CA: Sage.

Eck, J. E., & Spelman, W. (1987). Who ya gonna call? The police as problem busters. *Crime and Delinquency, 33,* 31-52.

Enter the Muslims, exit the drug dealers. (1989, February 17). *Philadelphia Inquirer.*

Esbensen, F., & Huizinga, D. (1993). Gangs, drugs, and delinquency in a survey of urban youth. *Criminology, 31,* 565-587.

Fagan, J. (1988). *The social organization of drug use and drug dealing among urban gangs.* New York: John Jay College of Criminal Justice.

Fagan, J. (1992). Drug selling and licit income in distressed neighborhoods: The economic lives of street level drug users and dealers. In A. V. Harrell & G. E. Petersen (Eds.), *Drugs, crime, and social isolation* (pp. 99-146). Washington, DC: Urban Institute.

Fagan, J., & Chin, K. (1990). Violence as regulation and social control in the distribution of crack. In M. De la Rosa, E. Y. Lambert, & B. Gropper (Eds.), *Drugs and violence: Causes, correlates, and consequences* (NIDA Research Monograph, 103, pp. 8-43). Washington, DC: Government Printing Office.

Fattah, E. A. (1991). *Understanding criminal victimization.* Scarborough, Ontario: Prentice Hall Canada.

Fattah, E. A. (1993). The rational choice/opportunity perspectives as a vehicle for integrating criminological and victimological theories. In R. V. Clarke & M. Felson (Eds.), *Routine activity and rational choice* (pp. 225-258). New Brunswick, NJ: Transaction Books.

Fischer, C. S., Jackson, R. M., Steuve, C. A., Gerson, K., & Jones, L. M. (1977). *Network and places: Social relations in the urban setting.* New York: Free Press.

Fowler, F. J., & Mangione, T. W. (1986). A three-pronged effort to reduce crime and fear of crime: The Hartford experiment. In D. P. Rosenbaum (Ed.), *Community crime prevention: Does it work?* (pp. 87-108). Beverly Hills, CA: Sage.

Freeman, R. B., & Holzer, H. (1986). *The black youth employment crisis.* Chicago: University of Chicago Press.

Gandossy, R. P., Williams, J. R., Cohen, J., & Harwood, H. J. (1980). *Drugs and crime: A survey and analysis of the literature.* Washington, DC: National Institute of Justice.

Garbarino, J., Kostelny, K., & Dubrow, N. (1991). *No place to be a child*. Lexington, MA: Lexington Books.

Garofalo, J., & McLeod, M. (1988). *Improving the effectiveness of neighborhood watch programs*. Unpublished report to the National Institute of Justice from the Hindelang Criminal Justice Research Center, State University of New York at Albany.

Gerstenzang, J., & Jehl, D. (1989, December 8). Bush praises citizenry for taking back park. *Los Angeles Times*, Sec. A, p. 49.

Gibbs, J. T. (1988). *Young, black, and male in America: An endangered species*. Dover, MA: Auburn House.

Goerdt, J., & Martin, J. A. (1989, Fall). The impact of drug cases on case processing in urban trial courts. *State Court Journal, 13*, 4-12.

Goldstein, H. (1990). *Problem-oriented policing*. New York: McGraw-Hill.

Goldstein, P. J. (1985). The drugs/violence nexus. *Journal of Drug Issues, 15*, 493-506.

Gottfredson, M., & Hindelang, M. (1979). A study of the behavior of law. *American Sociological Review, 44*, 3-17.

Gravois, J., & Lanterman, K. (1989, December 8). Bush to Houston: Good job. *Houston Post*, Sec. A, pp. 1, 19.

Green, L. A. (1996). *Policing places with drug problems*. Thousand Oaks, CA: Sage.

Greenberg, S., Rohe, W. M., & Williams, J. R. (1982). *Safe and secure neighborhoods: Physical characteristics and informal territorial control in high and low crime neighborhoods*. Washington, DC: National Institute of Justice.

Greenberg, S. W., Rohe, W. M., & Williams, J. R. (1985). *Informal citizen action and crime prevention at the neighborhood level: Synthesis and assessment of the research*. Washington, DC: National Institute of Justice.

Greene, J. R., & McLaughlin, E. (1993). Facilitating communities through police work: Drug problem solving and neighborhood involvement in Philadelphia. In R. C. Davis, A. J. Lurigio, & D. P. Rosenbaum (Eds.), *Drugs and the community* (pp. 141-161). Springfield, IL: Charles C Thomas.

Greene, J. R., & Taylor, R. B. (1988). Community-based policing and foot patrol: Issues of theory and evaluation. In J. R. Greene & S. D. Mostrofski (Eds.), *Community policing: Rhetoric or reality?* (pp. 195-224). New York: Praeger.

Hagedorn, J. M. (1994). Neighborhoods, markets, and gang drug organization. *Journal of Research in Crime and Delinquency, 31*, 264-294.

Hamid, A. (1990). The political economy of crack-related violence. *Contemporary Drug Problems, 17*, 31-78.

Hawkins, J., & Lam, T. (1987). Teacher practices, social development, and delinquency. In J. Burchard & S. Burchard (Eds.), *The prevention of delinquent behavior* (pp. 241-274). Beverly Hills, CA: Sage.

Hayeslip, D. W. (1989). Local-level drug enforcement: New strategies. *NIJ Reports, 213*, 2-6. Washington, DC: U.S. Department of Justice, National Institute of Justice.

Heinzelmann, F. (1981). Crime prevention and the physical environment. In D. A. Lewis (Ed.), *Reactions to crime* (pp. 87-102). Beverly Hills, CA: Sage.

Heinzelmann, F. (1983). Crime prevention from a community perspective. In Center for Responsive Governance (Ed.), *Community crime prevention* (pp. 17-24). Washington, DC: Editor.

Heller, N. B., Stenzel, W. W., & Gill, A. (1975). *National Evaluation Program—Phase I summary report: Operation Identification Projects*. Washington, DC: Law Enforcement Assistance Administration.

Henig, J. R. (1982). *Neighborhood mobilization*. New Brunswick, NJ: Rutgers University Press.

Holmes, S. A. (1989, November 15). Community shrinks from crack embrace. *New York Times*, Sec. B, pp. 1, 9.

Horacek, H., Ramey, D., Campbell, F., Hoffman, K., & Fletcher, R. (1987). Preventing school failure and assessing early intervention with high-risk children. *Journal of the American Academy of Child and Adolescent Psychiatry, 26*, 758-763.

Hunt, L. G., & Chambers, C. D. (1976). *The heroin epidemic: A study of heroin use in the U.S. 1965-75* (Part 2). Holliswood, NY: Spectrum.

Hunter, A. J. (1978, November). *Symbols of incivility: Social disorder and fear of crime in urban neighborhoods.* Paper presented at the annual meeting of the American Society of Criminology, Dallas.

Inciardi, J. A. (1980). Youth, drugs, and street crime. In F. R. Scarpitti & S. K. Datesman (Eds.), *Drugs and the youth culture* (pp. 175-203). Beverly Hills, CA: Sage.

Inciardi, J. A. (1986). *The war on drugs: Heroin, cocaine, crime, and public policy.* Palo Alto, CA: Mayfield.

Innes, C. A. (1988). *Drug use and crime.* Washington, DC: U.S. Department of Justice, Bureau of Justice Statistics.

International Training, Research, and Evaluation Council. (1977). *National Evaluation Program—Phase I summary report: Crime prevention security surveys.* Washington, DC: Law Enforcement Assistance Administration.

Jacobs, J. (1961). *Death and life of great American cities.* New York: Vintage.

Joe, K. (1992, November). *The social organization of Asian gangs, the Chinese mafia, and organized crime on the West Coast.* Paper presented at the annual meeting of the American Society of Criminology, New Orleans.

Johnson, B. D., Kaplan, M., & Schmeidler, J. (1990). Days with drug distribution: Which drugs? How many transactions? With what returns? In R. Weisheit (Ed.), *Drugs, crime, and the criminal justice system* (pp. 193-214). Cincinnati, OH: Anderson.

Johnson, B. D., Williams, T., Dei, K. A., & Sanabria, H. (1990). Drug abuse in the inner city: Impact on hard-drug users and the community. In M. Tonry & J. Q. Wilson (Eds.), *Drugs and crime* (pp. 9-68). Chicago: University of Chicago Press.

Kates, N. D. (1990). *REACH: Fighting crack and crime in Pilgrim Village, Detroit.* Draft report of the Kennedy School of Government Case Program, Harvard University.

Kelling, G. L., & Moore, M. (1988). From political reform to community: The evolving strategy of police. In J. R. Greene & S. D. Mastrofski (Eds.), *Community policing: Rhetoric or reality?* (pp. 3-26). New York: Praeger.

Kleiman, M. (1988). Crackdowns: The effects of intensive enforcement on retail heroin dealing. In M. Chaiken (Ed.), *Street-level drug enforcement: Examining the issues* (pp. 27-38). Washington, DC: National Institute of Justice.

Kleiman, M. A. R. (1992). *Against excess.* New York: Basic Books.

Kleiman, M. A. R., & Smith, K. D. (1990). State and local drug enforcement: In search of a strategy. In M. Tonry & J. Q. Wilson (Eds.), *Drugs and crime* (pp. 69-108). Chicago: University of Chicago Press.

Klitzner, M. (1993). A public health/dynamic systems approach to community-wide alcohol and other drug initiatives. In R. C. Davis, A. Lurigio, & D. P. Rosenbaum (Eds.), *Drugs and the community* (pp. 201-224). Springfield, IL: Charles C Thomas.

Klitzner, M., Stewart, K., Fisher, D., Carmona, M., Diggs, G., Stein-Seroussi, A., & Des Jarlais, D. (1992). *Final report on the planning phase of fighting back: Community initiatives to reduce the demand for illegal drugs and alcohol.* Baltimore, MD: Pacific Institute for Research and Evaluation.

Krosnick, J., & Judd, C. (1986). Transitions in social influence at adolescence: Who induces cigarette smoking? *Developmental Psychology, 18,* 359-68.

Lab, S. P. (1992). *Crime prevention: Approaches, practices, and evaluations.* Cincinnati, OH: Anderson.

Latane, B., & Darley, J. (1969). Bystander apathy. *American Scientist, 57,* 244-268.

Lavrakas, P. J. (1981). On households. In D. A. Lewis (Ed.), *Reactions to crime* (pp. 67-86). Beverly Hills, CA: Sage.

Lavrakas, P. J. (1985). Citizen self-help and neighborhood crime prevention. In L. Curtis (Ed.), *American violence and public policy* (pp. 47-56). New Haven, CT: Yale University Press.

Lavrakas, P. J. (1988). *Richard Clark and associates: A survey of black Americans.* Evanston, IL: Northwestern University Survey Laboratory.

Lavrakas, P. J., & Kushmuk, J. W. (1986). Evaluating crime prevention through environmental design: The Portland Commercial Demonstration Project. In D. P. Rosenbaum (Ed.), *Community crime prevention: Does it work?* (pp. 202-227). Beverly Hills, CA: Sage.

Lavrakas, P. J., & Lewis, D. A. (1980, July). The conceptualization and measurement of citizens' crime prevention behaviors. *Journal of Research in Crime and Delinquency, 17,* 254-272.

Lavrakas, P. J., & Rosenbaum, D. P. (1989). *Crime prevention beliefs, policies, and practices of chief law enforcement executives: Results of a national survey.* Evanston, IL: Northwestern University Survey Laboratory.

Lewis, D. A., & Salem, G. (1981). Community crime prevention: An analysis of a developing perspective. *Crime and Delinquency, 27,* 405-421.

Lockhard, J. L., Duncan, J. T., & Brenner, R. N. (1978). *Directory of community crime prevention programs: National and state levels.* Washington, DC: Law Enforcement Assistance Administration.

Lundberg, K. (1990). *The Philadelphia anti-drug coalition.* Draft report of the Kennedy School of Government Case Program, Harvard University.

Lurigio, A., Davis, R., Regulus, T., Gwisada, V., Popkin, S., Dantzker, M., Smith, B., & Ouellet, A. (1993). *An evaluation of the Cook County State Attorney's Office Narcotics Nuisance Abatement Program.* Chicago: Loyola University Department of Criminal Justice.

Maccoby, E., Johnson, J., & Church, R. (1958). Community integration and social control of juvenile delinquency. *Journal of Social Issues, 14,* 38-51.

Martens, F. T. (1988, May). *Narcotics enforcement: What are the goals and do they conflict?* Paper presented at the Organized Crime Narcotics Enforcement Symposium, Villanova University.

Mieczkowski, T. (1990). Drugs, crime, and the failure of American organized crime models. *International Journal of Comparative and Applied Criminal Justice, 14,* 97-106.

Milwaukee Police Department. (1994, March 22). [Internal memorandum].

Moore, M. M. (1973). Achieving discrimination on the effective price of heroin. *American Economic Review, 63*(2), 270-277.

Moore, M. M. (1976). *Buy and bust: The effective regulation of an illicit market in heroin.* Lexington, MA: D. C. Heath.

Morgan, T. (1988, February 25). Moslem patrol helps cut crime in Brooklyn. *New York Times,* Sec. A, p. 3.

Murder zones. (1989, April 10). *U.S. News and World Report,* pp. 20-32.

Nadelman, E. A. (1988). The case for legalization. *Public Interest, 92,* 3-31.

National Center for Neighborhood Enterprise. (1990). *Not here you don't: Neighborhood groups fight back in the war on drugs.* Draft monograph of the National Center for Neighborhood Enterprise, Washington, DC.

National Institute of Justice. (1994). *Drug use forecasting study: Drugs and crime, 1990—Annual report.* Washington, DC: Author.

Newman, O. (1973). *Defensible space: Crime prevention through urban design.* New York: Collier.

Newman, O., & Franck, K. A. (1980). *Factors influencing crime and instability in urban housing developments.* Washington, DC: Government Printing Office.

Nurco, D. N., Ball, J. C., Shaffer, J. W., & Hanlon, T. E. (1985). The criminality of narcotics addicts. *Journal of Nervous and Mental Diseases, 173,* 94-102.

Nurco, D. N., Kinlock, T., & Balter, M. B. (1993). The severity of preaddiction criminal behavior among urban, male narcotic addicts and two nonaddicted control groups. *Journal of Research in Crime and Delinquency, 30,* 293-316.

Pati, A., McPherson, M., & Silloway, G. (1987). *The Minneapolis crime prevention experiment.* Washington, DC: Police Foundation.

Penning, M., & Barnes, G. (1982). Adolescent marijuana use: A review. *International Journal of Addictions, 17,* 749-791.

Perkins, D., Florin, P., Rich, R., Wandersman, A., & Chavis, D. (1990). Participation and the social and physical environment of residential blocks: Crime and community context. *American Journal of Community Psychology, 18,* 83-115.

Phillips, C. (1989, September 6). Houston group battles, reclaims park. *Wall Street Journal,* Sec. A, pp. 10-11.

Piliavin, J., Doridio, J., Gaertner, S., & Clark, R. (1981). *Emergency intervention.* New York: Academic Press.

Podolefsky, A , & DuBow, F. (1981). *Strategies for community crime prevention.* Springfield, IL: Charles C Thomas.

Police swarm over Mayfair area. (1988, April 23). *Washington Post.*

Pothier, D. (1987, March 11). Department's "reputation grew uglier" over the years. *Philadelphia Inquirer.*

Powers, S. A. (1990). *Community responses to drugs.* Draft report of the Vera Institute of Justice, New York.

Powers, S. A. (1993). Community responses to drugs: Manhattan and Brooklyn case studies. In R. D. Davis, A. L. Lurigio, & D. P. Rosenbaum (Eds.), *Drugs and the community* (pp. 106-122). Springfield, IL: Charles C Thomas.

Press, A. (1987). *Piecing together New York's criminal justice system: The response to crack.* New York: New York Bar Association.

Rengert, G. F. (1990). *Drug marketing, property crime, and neighborhood viability: Organized crime connections.* Report to the Pennsylvania Commission by the Department of Criminal Justice, Temple University.

Reuter, P., & Haaga, J. (1989). *The organization of high-level drug markets: An exploratory study.* Santa Monica, CA: RAND.

Reuter, P., Haaga, J., Murphey, P., & Praskac, A. (1988). *Drug use and drug programs in the Washington metropolitan area* (Report No. R-3655-GWRC). Santa Monica, CA: RAND.

Reuter, P., & Kleiman, M. A. R. (1986). Risks and prices: An economic analysis of drug enforcement. In M. Tonry & N. Morris (Eds.), *Crime and justice* (pp. 289-340). Chicago: University of Chicago Press.

Reuter, P., MacCoun, R., & Murphy, P. (1990). *Money from crime: A study of the economics of drug dealing in Washington, DC.* Santa Monica, CA: RAND.

Roehl, J. A. (1995). *National process evaluation of the weed and seed initiative* (Draft report). Washington, DC: National Institute of Justice.

Roehl, J. A., Wong, H., Huitt, R., & Capowich, G. E. (1995). *A national assessment of community-based anti-drug initiatives: Final report.* Pacific Grove, CA: Institute for Social Analysis.

Ropers, R. H. (1988). *The invisible homeless: A new urban ecology.* New York: Insight.

Rosenbaum, D. P. (1983, August). *Scaring people into crime prevention: The results of a randomized experiment.* Paper presented at the 91st annual convention of the American Psychological Association, Anaheim, CA.

Rosenbaum, D. P. (1986). The problem of crime control. In D. P. Rosenbaum (Ed.), *Community crime prevention: Does it work?* (pp. 11-18). Beverly Hills, CA: Sage.

Rosenbaum, D. P. (1987). The theory and research behind neighborhood watch: Is it a sound fear and crime reduction strategy? *Crime and Delinquency, 23,* 103-134.

Rosenbaum, D. P. (1988). Community crime prevention: A review and synthesis of the literature. *Justice Quarterly, 5,* 323-395.

Rosenbaum, D. P. (1993). Civil liberties and aggressive enforcement: Balancing the rights of individuals and society in the drug war. In R. C. Davis, A. J. Lurigio, & D. P. Rosenbaum (Eds.), *Drugs and the community* (pp. 55-84). Springfield, IL: Charles C Thomas.

Rosenbaum, D. P., Bennett, S. F., Lindsay, B., & Wilkinson, D. L. (1994). *Community responses to drug abuse: A program evaluation.* Washington, DC: National Institute of Justice.

Rosenbaum, D. P., Bennett, S. F., Lindsay, B. D., Wilkinson, D. L., Davis, B., Taranowski, C., & Lavrakas, P. J. (1992). *Ten case studies: The community responses to drug abuse* (National Demonstration Program Final Process Evaluation Report, Vol. 2). Washington, DC: National Institute of Justice.

Rosenbaum, D. P., & Lavrakas, P. J. (1993, November). *The impact of voluntary community organizations on communities: A test of the implant hypothesis.* Paper presented at the annual meeting of the American Society of Criminology, Phoenix, AZ.

Rosenbaum, D. P., Lewis, D. A., & Grant, J. A. (1985). *The impact of community crime prevention programs in Chicago: Can neighborhood organizations make a difference?* Evanston, IL: Northwestern University, Center for Urban Affairs and Policy Research.

Rosenbaum, D. P., Lewis, D. A., & Grant, J. A. (1986). Neighborhood-based crime prevention: Assessing the efficacy of community organizing in Chicago. In D. P.

Rosenbaum (Ed.), *Community crime prevention: Does it work?* (pp. 109-136). Beverly Hills, CA: Sage.

Rosenbaum, D. P., & Lurigio, A. J. (1994). An inside look at community policing reform: Definitions, organizational changes, and evaluation findings. *Crime and Delinquency, 40,* 299-314.

Rosenbaum, D., Lurigio, A., & Lavrakas, P. (1989). Enhancing citizen participation and solving serious crime: A national evaluation of crime stoppers programs. *Crime and Delinquency, 35,* 401-420.

Sadd, S., & Grinc, R. M. (1993). The effects of drug use and sales on three urban communities. In R. C. Davis, A. J. Lurigio, & D. P. Rosenbaum (Eds.), *Drugs and the community* (pp. 175-197). Springfield, IL: Charles C Thomas.

Schmalleger, F. (1995). *Criminal justice today.* Englewood Cliffs, NJ: Prentice Hall.

Schneider, A. L. (1986). Neighborhood-based antiburglary strategies: An analysis of public and private benefits from the Portland program. In D. P. Rosenbaum (Ed.), *Community crime prevention: Does it work?* (pp. 68-86). Beverly Hills, CA: Sage.

Schneider, A. L., Burcart, J., & Wilson, L. (1976). The role of attitudes in the decision to report crimes to the police. In W. MacDonald (Ed.), *Criminal justice and the victim* (pp. 63-81). Beverly Hills, CA: Sage.

Shedler, J., & Block, J. (1990). Adolescent drug use and psychological health: A longitudinal inquiry. *American Psychologist, 45,* 612-630.

Sherman, L. W. (1990). Police crackdowns: Initial and residual deterrence. In M. Tonry & N. Morris (Eds.), *Crime and justice: A review of research* (pp. 1-48). Chicago: University of Chicago Press.

Sherman, L. W. (1992, March). *Kansas City drug market analysis: DRAGNET.* Paper presented at the annual meeting of the Academy of Criminal Justice Sciences, Pittsburgh, PA.

Sherman, L., Gartin, P., & Buerger, M. E. (1989). Hot spots of predatory crime: Routine activities and the criminology of place. *Criminology, 27,* 27-55.

Siegel, R. (1982). Cocaine smoking. *Journal of Psychoactive Drugs, 14,* 277-359.

Simon, H. (1991). *United neighbors against drugs.* Report of the Kennedy School of Government Case Program, Harvard University.

Sizer, T. (1992). *Horace's school: Redesigning the American high school.* New York: Houghton Mifflin.

Skogan, W. G. (1988). Community organizations and crime. In M. Tonry & N. Morris (Eds.), *Crime and justice* (pp. 39-78). Chicago: University of Chicago Press.

Skogan, W. G. (1989). Communities, crime, and neighborhood organization. *Crime and Delinquency, 35,* 437-457.

Skogan, W. G. (1990). *Disorder and decline: Crime and the spiral to decay in American cities.* New York: Free Press.

Skogan, W. G., & Antunes, G. (1979). Information, apprehension and deterrence: Exploring the limits of police productivity. *Journal of Criminal Justice, 10,* 217-242.

Skogan, W. G., & Maxfield, M. G. (1981). *Coping with crime.* Beverly Hills, CA: Sage.

Skolnick, J. H. (1990). The social structure of street drug dealing. *American Journal of Police, 9,* 1-41.

Skolnik, J. H., & Bayley, D. (1986). *The new blue line.* New York: Free Press.

Smith, B. E., Davis, R. C., & Goretsky, S. R. (1991). *Strategies for courts to cope with the caseload pressures of drug cases.* Washington, DC: American Bar Association.

Smith, B. E., Davis, R. C., Hillenbrand, S. W., & Goretsky, S. R. (1992). *Ridding neighborhoods of drug houses in the private sector.* Washington, DC: American Bar Association.

Smith, B. E., Lurigio, A., Davis, R. C., Goretsky-Elstein, S., & Popkin, S. (1994). Burning the midnight oil: An examination of Cook County's night drug court. *Justice System Journal, 17,* 41-52.

Some residents being won over by the enemy in the D.C. drug war. (1989, August 13). *Washington Post.*

Sparks, R., Genn, H., & Dodd, D. (1977). *Surveying victims: A study of the measurement of criminal victimization, perception of crime, and attitudes toward criminal justice.* New York: John Wiley.

Spelman, W., & Brown, D. K. (1984). *Calling the police: Citizen reporting of serious crime.* Washington, DC: Government Printing Office.

Suttles, G. (1972). *The social construction of communities.* Chicago: University of Chicago Press.

Sviridoff, M., & Hillsman, S. T. (1994). Assessing the community effects of Tactical Narcotics Teams. In D. L. MacKenzie & C. D. Uchida (Eds.), *Drugs and crime: Evaluating public policy initiatives* (pp. 114-128). Thousand Oaks, CA: Sage.

Taxman, F. S., & McEwen, T. (1994). *The drug market analysis project: Defining markets and effective law enforcement practices.* Alexandria, VA: Institute for Law and Justice.

Taylor, C. (1990). *Dangerous society.* East Lansing: Michigan State University Press.

Taylor, R. B., & Gottfredson, S. (1987). Environmental design, crime, and prevention. In A. Reiss & M. Tonry (Eds.), *Communities and crime* (pp. 387-416). Chicago: University of Chicago Press.

Taylor, R. B., Gottfredson, S. D., & Brower, S. (1981). Territorial cognitions and social climate in urban neighborhoods. *Basic and Applied Social Psychology, 2,* 289-303.

Threats of death, maiming muzzle witnesses in area drug trials. (1989, August 20). *Washington Post.*

Tien, J. M., & Rich, T. F. (1994). The Hartford COMPASS Program: Experiences with a Weed- and Seed-Related Program. In D. P. Rosenbaum (Ed.), *The challenge of community policing: Testing the promises* (pp. 192-208). Thousand Oaks, CA: Sage.

Tien, J., Rich, T., Shell, M., Larson, R., & Donnelly, J. (1993). *COMPASS: A drug market analysis program.* Final report of the Hartford, CT, Police Department to the National Institute of Justice.

Tonry, M. (1994). Racial politics, racial disparities, and the war on crime. *Crime and Delinquency, 40,* 475-494.

Trebach, A. S., & Inciardi, J. A. (1993). *Legalize it? Debating American drug policy.* Washington, DC: American University Press.

Uchida, C. D., & Forst, B. (1994). Controlling street-level drug trafficking: Professional and community policing approaches. In D. L. MacKenzie & C. D. Uchida (Eds.), *Drugs and crime: Evaluating public policy initiatives* (pp. 77-94). Thousand Oaks, CA: Sage.

Uchida, C. D., Forst, B., & Annan, S. O. (1992). *Modern policing and the control of illegal drugs: Testing new strategies in two American cities.* Washington, DC: U.S. Department of Justice, National Institute of Justice.

U.S. Department of Justice. (1981). *Criminal victimization in the United States, 1979.* Washington, DC: Department of Justice Statistics.

Waldorf, D., & Lauderback, D. (1993). *Gang drug sales in San Francisco: Organized or freelance?* Unpublished paper of the Institute for Scientific Analysis, Alameda, CA.

Walker, S. (1992). *The police in America.* New York: McGraw-Hill.

Waller, I., & Okihiro, N. (1978). *Burglary: The victim and the public.* Toronto: University of Toronto Press.

Weingart, S. (1993). A typology of community responses to drugs. In R. C. Davis, A. Lurigio, & D. P. Rosenbaum (Eds.), *Drugs and the community* (pp. 85-105). Springfield, IL: Charles C Thomas.

Weingart, S. N., Hartmann, F. X., & Osborne, D. (1992). *Lessons learned: Case studies of the initiation and maintenance of the community response to drugs.* Report of the Kennedy School, Harvard University, to the National Institute of Justice.

Weingart, S. N., Hartmann, F. X., & Osborne, D. (1994, October). *Case studies of community anti-drug efforts—NIJ Research in Brief.* Washington, DC: National Institute of Justice.

Weisburd, D. L., & Green, L. (1994). Defining the drug market: The case of the Jersey City DMAP system. In D. L. MacKenzie & C. D. Uchida (Eds.), *Drugs and crime: Evaluating public policy initiatives* (pp. 61-76). Thousand Oaks, CA: Sage.

Weisburd, D. L., & Green, L. (1995). *Policing hot spots: The Jersey City DMA experiment.* Manuscript submitted for publication.

White House. (1995). *National drug control strategy: Strengthening communities' response to drugs and crime.* Washington, DC: Government Printing Office.

Wilson, J. Q., & Kelling, G. (1982, February 29). Broken windows. *Atlantic Monthly, 38,* 46-52.

Wilson, J. W. (1978). *The investigators.* New York: Free Press.

Winkel, F. W. (1987). Response generalization in crime prevention campaigns: An experiment. *British Journal of Criminology, 27,* 155-174.

Wolfgang, M. E., & Ferracuti, F. (1967). *The subculture of violence: Toward an integrated theory in criminology.* London: Tavistock.

Worden, R. E., Bynum, T. S., & Frank, J. (1994). Police crackdowns on drug abuse and trafficking. In D. L. MacKenzie & C. D. Uchida (Eds.), *Drugs and crime: Evaluating public policy initiatives* (pp. 95-113). Thousand Oaks, CA: Sage.

Yin, R. K. (1979). What is citizen crime prevention? In Law Enforcement Assistance Administration (Ed.), *Review of criminal justice evaluation: 1978* (pp. 72-85). Washington, DC: Editor.

Yin, R. K., Vogel, M. E., & Chaiken, J. M. (1977). *National Evaluation Program—Phase I summary report: Citizen patrol projects.* Washington, DC: Law Enforcement Assistance Administration.

Zimmer, L. (1990). Proactive policing against street-level drug trafficking. *American Journal of Police, 9,* 43-74.

Index

About the Authors

Robert C. Davis is Senior Research Associate for Victim Services, New York, and a consultant to the American Bar Association. His research interests include community anticrime organizations, crime victims, domestic violence, and criminal courts. He has coedited the books *Drugs and the Community* and *Victims of Crime: Problems, Policies, and Programs* and has authored numerous journal articles and book chapters on these topics. He lives in Princeton, New Jersey, with his wife Patricia and children Caitlin and Jennifer.

Arthur J. Lurigio received his doctorate in social psychology from Loyola University in Chicago. He was formerly an Assistant Professor of Psychology and Urban Affairs at Northwestern University and is now an Associate Professor of Criminal Justice at Loyola University. He is also the Director of Research for the Cook County Adult Probation Department. He has many, varied research interests, including the psychological effects of criminal victimization, intermediate sanctions, crime and mental disorders, drugs and communities, community policing, community crime prevention, and traditional organized crime. He has published extensively in all these areas. He lives in Chicago with his wife Colleen and his two children, Michael and Caitlin.